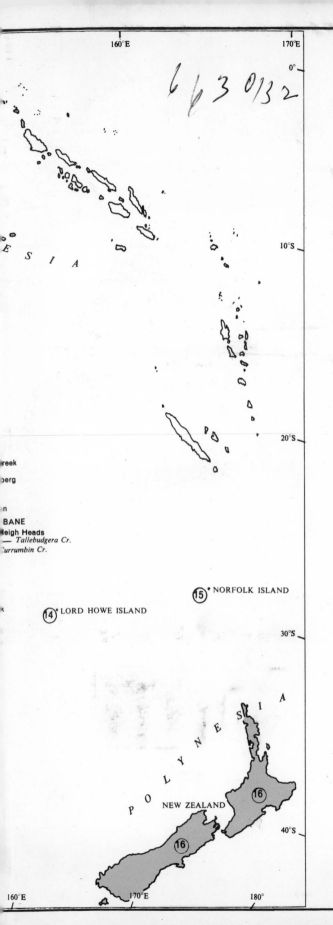

6 6 3 0 2

PO ~~OWL~~
Ninox ~~strenua~~

RUFOUS OWL
Ninox rufa

BARKING OWL
Ninox connivens

BOOBOOK OWL
Ninox novaeseelandiae

1	*Ninox novaeseelandiae plesseni*
2	*N. novaeseelandiae fusca*
3	*N. novaeseelandiae moae*
4	*N. novaeseelandiae cinnamomina*
5	*N. novaeseelandiae remigialis*
6	*N. novaeseelandiae pusilla*
7	*N. novaeseelandiae melvillensis*
8	*N. novaeseelandiae ocellata*
9	*N. novaeseelandiae rufigaster*
10	*N. novaeseelandiae boobook*
11	*N. novaeseelandiae lurida*
12	*N. novaeseelandiae halmaturina*
13	*N. novaeseelandiae leucopsis*
14	*N. novaeseelandiae albaria*
15	*N. novaeseelandiae undulata*
16	*N. novaeseelandiae novaeseelandiae*

Nightwatchmen of Bush and Plain

By the Same Author

We Breed the Platypus (1944)
Gliders of the Gum Trees (1947)
Talking of Animals (1956)
Living with Animals (1960)

Nightwatchmen of Bush and Plain

Australian owls and owl-like birds

DAVID FLEAY

M.B.E., B.Sc., Dip.Ed., C.M.Z.S.
(London and New York)

Taplinger Publishing Company
NEW YORK

First published in the United States in 1972 by
TAPLINGER PUBLISHING CO., INC.
New York, New York

Published simultaneously in the Dominion of Canada by
Burns & MacEachern Ltd., Ontario

Library of Congress Catalog Card Number: 73-171365

ISBN 0-8008-5560-4

To Jim Slater and Cecil Milne who in different places, at all times and in all weathers carried out routine without which there is no success. To Merv Goddard also — the incomparable climber whose nerves are made of steel.

Acknowledgements

Acknowledgment of assistance in the many aspects of compiling this publication is made to: Roy Goodisson, Esq. (formerly Womboota, N.S.W. now Kilsyth, Vic.); Mr Jack Woods, Director of the Queensland Museum and his staff; Eric Zillmann, Esq. (Gin Gin); Hugh Innes, Esq. (Walla); Primary Industries Department, Qld. for helpful permits for study; Stan Stirling, Esq. (Stratford, north Queensland); M. S. R. Sharland, Esq. (Hobart); Dr G. F. Mees, formerly of the Western Australian Museum—now of the Natural History Museum, Leiden, Holland; the *Emu*—official journal of the R.A.O.U.; the Botanic Museum and Herbarium, Brisbane, and Dr Gordon Williams, Director of Wild Life Service, New Zealand. I also thank Merv Goddard (Tenterfield, N.S.W.) for checking every statement with meticulous care, and all those good mates who staggered with me through the bush at all hours of days and nights of many years. Photographs reproduced in this book which are not specifically credited, were taken by the author.

Foreword

Every citizen in Australia owes a deep debt of gratitude to David Fleay for the most important work that he is carrying out, in opening our eyes to the unique fauna which exists on this vast island continent.

At an early age he discovered that the source of true happiness springs from the wonders of nature.

He instinctively knew that his life's work lay in pursuit of knowledge about our indigenous neighbours, the birds, animals, and reptiles of Australia.

His chosen way through life met with strong parental opposition. This difficulty he had to overcome, he then set out to lay firm foundations for his career by qualifying as a Bachelor of Science.

David Fleay's very great achievements are due to his courage, determination, perseverance, and sensitivity. *Nightwatchmen of Bush and Plain* is the result of over forty years of dedicated and immensely hard work, and at times danger and hardship. It has enabled him to acquire an ever closer understanding of the fauna of Australia, and their life cycles. He has made a special study of the birds which are nocturnal in mode of life.

What a thrill it is, in the quietness of the night, to hear the call of an owl. Many of us have longed to learn something of our neighbours who hunt under cover of darkness.

David Fleay, by his indefatigable field work, and his keen powers of observation, has greatly increased the scientific knowledge concerning the fauna of Australia. He has established magnificent sanctuaries where every facility is given to visitors to see, and learn, something of the wild life of our land.

The fascinating articles which he writes for our newspapers, and magazines, and his deeply interesting books, give to each one of us the opportunity to share his knowledge, and enjoyment, of the wonders of nature.

It is the responsibility of each one of us, to ensure that this priceless heritage, our wild life, is conserved for the joy of those who come after us.

HENRY ABEL SMITH

Sir Henry Abel Smith, K.C.M.G., K.C.V.O., D.S.O.,
Governor of Queensland, 1958–1966.

Barton Lodge,
Winkfield,
Windsor, U.K.
22 July, 1967.

Contents

Introduction

By virtue of their special eyesight, coupled with forward vision, on 'rubber' necks and soft noiseless flight, owls are not only birds of the darker hours but in Australia, particularly, they epitomize the mysterious continent itself. To me they have always been inseparable from their dream-time environments, moving as they do at a gentler period, when the very spirit of the land breathes in the quiet freshness amid the shadows of great bushlands and far-reaching plains under the cloak of night.

Voices of owls are therefore—to those who understand—much more than the conversation of nocturnal birds. They are an expression of atmosphere—scents and sounds and scenes of the fairyland night among the gum trees when so many creatures are on the move safe from the heat, the glare and the insecurity of revealing day.

In the mythology of ancient Greece Athene, the Goddess of Wisdom, was so impressed by the great eyes and solemn appearance of the owl that, having banished the mischievous crow, she honoured the night bird by making him her favourite among feathered creatures. In turn, 130 years ago, the name *Athene* was used as an early generic label for our Hawk Owls, now included in the genus *Ninox*.

In these days of great technological advances in so many fields, when cold scientific facts often cloud human expression of life's delightful natural aspects, I trust that, without sacrifice of accuracy on my part, not only the specially interested, but also 'the man in the street' may find this account readable.

It deals generally with all Australian owls within the two very different families of Hawk Owls (Strigidae) and Masked Owls

(Tytonidae) of the order Strigiformes (Nocturnal Birds of Prey), and less thoroughly with the continent's owl-like birds or Night-jars (families Podargidae, Aegothelidae and Caprimulgidae)—of the order Coraciiformes—so often confused with the genuine article.

Among unalterable facts, I have hoped to convey impressions of those times of happiness, excitement, inspiration and high hope that went with the pursuit of will o' the wisp nocturnal birds, for to me, owls recall the most wonderful journeys of my life. Along the moonpaths and under the stars, in fact, there is a world of intense and abiding interest known to few but wide open to all.

Be proud of things characteristically Australian and do make sure for the sake of the future that children in particular treat them with the respect they deserve.

D. H. Fleay

Chapter One

Early Exploration
of Powerful Owl Haunts

My father was one of the old school with a deep-rooted belief that, come what may, his sons, and particularly the elder one, who happened to be me, should follow in his footsteps.

To him there were no such trivia as child psychology or vocational guidance. Consequently, having left Ballarat Grammar School in late 1923 and having spent every spare moment of those early years rejoicing in neighbouring bushland, watching birds, chasing rabbits and altogether imagining myself a kind of junior partner of Messrs Burke and Wills, Captain Charles Sturt or Ned Kelly, I found myself to my intense dismay, apprenticed to Dad's pharmacy in the unromantic heart of Ballarat's business centre.

They were the days of few jobs and strict discipline and though my 'captivity' was to last only two and a half years, it seemed at the time that the world I knew had come to an end for ever. At five shillings weekly, I washed thousands of bottles in intensely cold water, dusted shelves and died a hundred deaths daily as a 'shrinking violet' selling fastidious ladies their favourite brands of powder. I didn't have the gumption to ask whether they wanted face, gun or bug!

From his eminence as Chairman of the Pharmacy Board of Victoria, Dad regarded my prospects as good, especially considering, through force of circumstance in his own case, that he had begun his career at the age of twelve earning two and sixpence weekly helping support his mother, younger brothers and sisters by picking seeds in the local botanical gardens.

To a 'non-conformist' sixteen-year-old, slightly handicapped by eighteen months of polio, devoted to the out-of-doors, and hyper-sensitive to atmosphere, this 'secure' roofed-in future appeared equally as bad as being buried alive. Little wonder I showed no promise and shone only at detecting and catching rats in the store shed. Occasionally we did brighten early morning hours by such experiments as heating sealed, water-filled tins, weighted with bricks, on the gas ring to discover the rocketing power of super-heated steam, and I did achieve some municipal notoriety by bringing about a huge bang with an unmerciful quantity of mixed sulphur and potassium chlorate, that practically blasted the ad-joining Carlyon's Hotel off its foundations.

That escapade almost brought me before Ballarat's City Court. Then of course the other apprentice and I discovered, and dispensed from a book, to the detriment of the sugar store, delightful recipes for Turkish delight, fudge and boiled lollies.

Into this dry, drab, eau-de-Cologne world of coloured bottles, ailing invalids and patent medicines shone, however, an unexpected ray of light destined eventually to lead to high adventure.

My father introduced me to an infrequent customer, a big bearded farmer named William Labbett, shopping for the day from his farm at Bullarook, an outlying easterly district some twelve miles distant. A long-time bushman, he noted my keen interest in his mention of wild life, and wombats in particular, in the deep forest of uninhabited range country in a giant triangle pointed by the townships of Ballan, Blackwood and Daylesford. His sug-gestion that we camp there some weekend never had a more eager taker, and so, without any realization on my part, fate took a hand in my introduction to a magnificent bird destined not only to influence the course of my life but, as the seasons came and went, to frustrate and elude me—yet ever fascinate—and remain con-stantly the most compelling interest ever to grip me in long years of the study of natural history.

All these decades later, this regal, austere, peculiarly Australian, Powerful Owl *(Ninox strenua)* giant of the continent's nocturnal birds of prey, epitome of solitude and the voice that expresses as no other the essence and grandeur of the mountain bushlands, is as fresh and exciting as the day I met it first forty-three years ago.

However, I must slow the gallop before we lose the horse!

On a drizzling Friday night in late autumn 1924, Mr Labbett and one of his sons took me to Bullarook in a T-model Ford. For once I had escaped Saturday morning and Sunday duty and early next day we set forth by horse and spring cart towards the Moorabool Reservoir to enter deep forest that lay beyond.

2

Used as I was to the poor, hungry, dried-out timber of Ballarat's immediate environs, suffering as it did and would for generations from the ravages of goldmining, the unbroken forest we now penetrated along fading rutted bullock tracks was a delightful surprise. The sturdy, plodding horse took us further and further into a world I felt I wanted to stay in forever. Here was an environment for which I felt the strongest affinity. It seemed the home of a past life and indeed that forest became a Mecca, not only in my young life, but also in that of close cobbers from that time on.

Immense manna gums grew along tree-fern and blackwood gullies towering above thickets of silver wattle, grading through swamp gums to splendid peppermint and stringybark eucalypts on the ridges. It was late in the day and quite a few miles inside this enchanted, scented bushland when we camped on an ancient clearing occupied in bygone years by a sawmilling plant.

Nature was gradually reclaiming the open space which was so far within the heavily-forested hills, that nothing but the faintest whistle of a faraway train wafted across from the outside world. There were no such things, then, as intruding planes of the regular airlines. On the far side of this exclusive, unspoiled spot, where obviously no one had worked for years, rose an abrupt tree-clad range with graceful old monarchs etched against the northern sky.

At the foot of the range bubbled a creek of clear, cold water, moving smoothly along between fern-covered banks and through dark minnow pools to join the Werribee River many miles further down. All around was the bush, the tall graceful trees of the deep forest with the 'cree-cree' calls of slow-winged Currawongs echoing back and forth from the grey-green wall above. From overhead, occasionally, burst the double shriek of swiftly flying Crimson Parrots, whilst Scrub Wrens fussed in the thick bracken fern and Grey Thrushes treated us to the magic of their mellow outbursts.

'It was always a great spot,' remarked Mr Labbett. 'I worked at this mill twenty years ago but we took very few of the trees.' Indeed, huge hollow logs in various stages of decay lay about the creek in many places—evidence of the timbermen's forgotten quest. The ancient leaf-covered tracks were obviously used nightly, now, as pads by sturdy, shuffling wombats.

Above the camp, the gully split in two, becoming wilder, steeper and more tangled with a profusion of forest litter, wattles, tree ferns and young saplings. I remember that it was about five o'clock by the time we'd unloaded—everything being very still and quite cold under an overcast sky, with fragrant wood smoke curling up from the fire.

Suddenly just then, there arose from one of the upper gullies a deep deliberate call, like the moo-ing of a cow and unlike anything I'd ever heard before.

I walked quietly closer to the point from which the sound appeared to have its origin, but although there were four or five double calls, the deep 'woof-woof', 'oo-hoo', 'walk-walk' or 'woo-hoo' ceased at my approach and was heard no more that night.

The sound itself was reminiscent of the 'mopoke' of the Boobook Owl but had great volume, and although Mr Labbett had heard it in past times, he was unsure what bird or animal was responsible. I had an idea that it might be the call of the Powerful Owl about which I had read, but could not be at all certain, since, from scanty information available in those days, the Powerful Owl was said to scream, uttering drawn-out hideous screeches. Literature mentioned no other calls—unless there was justification for them in the great John Gould's description of a voice 'like that of an ox'. You could see Powerful Owls mounted in museums but beyond that there was practically no information about these great birds at all.

That fascinating first trip to the Korweingeboora forest with the Labbetts whetted my appetite for more and it became a point of honour to run to earth whatever mystery creature was responsible for the weird and wonderful 'whoo-whoo' or 'woof-woof' calls in the gully.

With chosen mates, all of us mounted on 'pack horse' bicycles, we began a series of trips at any and every opportunity, irrespective of weather, which was mostly bad, whenever we could escape. Nearly always, with but a blanket apiece and limited food, we camped again and again in that same forest clearing. Winter time in icy frosts, we slept inside giant hollow logs or out between three or four fires—in spite of the heat—still having our hats frozen on our heads. Indeed it was no novelty to travel home, more dead than alive, through heavy snow in the bitter cold of pre-dawn darkness singing the song of Good King Wenceslas to begin (in my case) Monday morning duty at the pharmacy by 7.45 a.m.! Only the tang of fragrant gum smoke lingered on—not to mention the

Opposite: *Largest and most impressive Australian night bird, the Powerful Owl is an 'outside' percher, not sheltering inside hollow trees except when brooding eggs or owlets. A mighty hunter of fixed and regular habits.*

Powerful Owl in the neighbourhood of Springbrook, Queensland.

Powerful Owl beak-snapping as a threat to the intruder.

bruises acquired on one occasion when a startled wombat blundering downhill at speed in the darkness bulldozed me into a tangled heap!

Summer time, when we were lucky enough occasionally, to borrow an old grocer's van and a still more ancient, jibbing horse with a foul breath called 'Bill', we roasted in the blasting heat of north wind days or choked in bushfire smoke; but through it all, no one else ever intruded upon our private world of fact and fantasy, and a romance and strangeness beckoned always.

The second trip was fruitless as far as discovering the origin of the mysterious call was concerned, though it came to us during the night, haunting and remote far up on the ridge tops—particularly in the stillness of the earliest signs of dawn.

However, on the third expedition, immediately prior to piccaninny daylight, that elusive voice began in the same offshoot gully whence it had originally arisen. It was no trouble to get going as we slept—full marching order—in 'boots and spurs', hat and jacket. Following a quiet stalk, I eventually got close enough to realize that the deep 'woo-hoo' was emanating from upper branches of a large blackwood tree right in the floor of the gully. Then came the realization in growing daylight that I was gazing directly at a now perfectly quiet, and entirely motionless, giant of an owl. I'd never seen anything larger than the little Boobook, but this enormous, upright, brown fellow with strongly barred chest and abdomen, staring haughtily and unblinkingly at me from great orange eyes, seemed at least two feet high. He was the most aloof impressive thing of his kind I had ever seen.

As I moved slowly below the tree, a piercing stare followed my every movement. Below him on the ground were innumerable bones and quite a collection of fresh, parcelled-up fur pellets, obviously disgorged from meals over a lengthy period.

This, then, was a regular perch. No other bird was seen and on other visits of inspection, this acquaintance of future seasons was not always there. However, for the first time in my life, I'd come across a Powerful Owl in its natural state and the event was momentous. Never had I seen such a colossal, aristocratic and altogether magnificent hunting bird.

To find out more about Powerful Owls was bird-observing under difficulties. Remember, we had first of all to push cycles for thirty-five miles, lugging them in the later stages along rough timber-strewn bullock tracks to reach our operational area. But that was the beauty of trips in those days. We were part of our surroundings and everything about us had its particular impact. The world was full of wonder and delight.

There were many other denizens of this lovely forest and during trips, particularly in summer time, it was vast entertainment to wait after dark under the towering dead trees which projected gaunt and majestic against the sky. As we watched in the stillness of evening, the round moon would rise red in smoky haze and cast strange shadows in the stately aisles of the tall gum trunks.

In certain of these lofty eucalypts, the dusky possum gliders had their homes. These furry giants amongst so-called 'flying squirrels' measured three feet in length from nose to tail tip and by day slept in the hollows of the high timber.

In the moonlight, we watched them saunter to the ends of high branches, gather themselves tightly and leap forth to glide grace-fully down and away with long tails streaming behind. They alighted on trunks of other trees, low down with an upward sweep and with a decided 'clop'. The animals gave vent to shrill cries, keeping in touch as they moved about feeding on the leafy branch tips of such favourite species as the broad-leaved peppermint, manna and swamp gums.

Ring-tailed possums, also, were moderately numerous in the gullies, constructing nests amid dense growth. It seemed, when in-vestigating the fur and bones lying below the known favourite perch of the Powerful Owl, that our 'strongman' hunter was in the habit of preying upon both of these species.

By no means did we confine our investigations to the immediate sawmill area but penetrated the forest in all directions within a radius of ten miles, often drinking mineral water from a bubbling spring we discovered by accident.

Two elderly brothers by the name of Smith conducted a euca-lyptus distillery back along an offshoot track to Korweingeboora, and apart from the tiny hotel at Spargo Creek, their contraption of boilers, pipes and old galvanised iron was the only sign of habitation in a local, rather extensive, peppermint forest. They had dwelt in the same spot for most of their lives and were redolent, as was everything else about their Heath Robinson outfit, of eucalyptus oil. These undernourished distillers who, if there is any truth in the use of eucalyptus oil as the panegyric for chills and all ills, should never have suffered as they did from colds, spoke in some awe of blood-curdling screams they had heard on odd occasions.

6

Naturally we, in our young enthusiasm, and with the limited knowledge available from current bird books, assumed of course that they had been listening to Powerful Owls. They went so far as to assure us that the sound caused dogs to slink under beds and horses to bolt.

From the centre of this distillery at 10 p.m. one night, we heard a Powerful Owl calling on a range top perhaps a mile away. Foolishly, we blundered off across hill and dale to try and locate the bird, becoming thoroughly lost in the process. The building of an all-night fire with the consequence of being dangerously stung in the process by at least forty robust bulldog ants irritated at having their nest log dragged up in the middle of the night, made it an evening never to be forgotten. As a matter of fact, becoming bushed and spending the night cold, wet, muddy, miserable and very, very hungry became quite commonplace. It is no wonder I cannot forget Powerful Owls. That slow deep 'woo-hoo' wafting so far in darker hours from my own birds here in Queensland now, takes me back like Paterson's drover's horse to older days as nothing else could ever do.

At all events, the Smith brothers spoke of hearing the deliberate double call in a certain gully about a mile distant from their hut. By dint of gradual elimination, we eventually pinpointed another perching spot here to find a second Powerful Owl roosting in yet another blackwood tree. Once again bones, fur and thick creamy whitewash indicated that we had a regular location.

The Smith brothers, who carried, as mentioned, such a powerful impregnation of their product that in the dark you knew when they were coming without seeing them, were definite in assuring us that this bird had called from that particular gully, on and off, for a good thirty years. I could well believe it for our new discovery appeared not only thoroughly mature but a big, dark bird of austere appearance and tremendous dignity, while older skeletal debris below the tree was green and mossy with age.

All in all, and off and on, during these intermittent trips over five years of the mid-twenties, we traversed that forest with diligent enthusiasm to locate only one other Powerful Owl in the whole territory.

Not once, strange to say, did we come across two owls together nor did we get any indication of nesting nor any sign of parents with young, and never at all did we hear a scream. It was all very, very, frustrating and it seemed that in our search for knowledge we were up against a baffling state of affairs. Nevertheless, lots of other creatures provided fascinating studies.

Here we caught our first wombats—in one case digging at a single burrow for a whole week—blocking the excavation at nights and continuing during the days that followed. But that is a different story altogether.

In 1926, having left the pharmacy in Ballarat with no regrets at being a total failure, I became, thanks to the assistance of my old headmaster at Ballarat Grammar School (E. V. Butler, Esq., M.A.) a junior master supervising the smaller boys at the old school. Not far from here, near the shores of Lake Wendouree and adjoining the Botanical Gardens, stood a small and quite delightful zoo, a bequest from Ben Jahn, a retired local business man.

The Curator, well-meaning, but not particularly well-informed, was friendly though unhelpful to young enthusiasts like myself. Who could blame him? Even in these advanced days I find that youngsters bristling with ideas can be a trifle wearing!

However, imagine my utter amazement on visiting the Ballarat Zoo in November 1926 to find a large, downy and obviously young owl sitting forlorn and sick on a perch over green slimy water in a former water-rat pen. From size it could be nothing else but a Powerful Owl, though the Curator referred to it without interest merely as an Australian 'howl'. It appeared that timber-getters at Mount Cole near Beaufort, Victoria, a section of the Dividing Range some forty miles west of Ballarat, had felled a hollow tree in a remote gully discovering this bird and another which failed to survive the crash.

So there before my eyes sat the most unbelievable treasure I could possibly imagine—a baby Powerful Owl, unrecognized and un-valued by the Zoo authorities and doomed to die unless something was done, and done quickly indeed.

Now, quite a number of bush creatures were housed at our home in Armstrong Street, North Ballarat, so I listed a number of attractive exhibits and begged my father to do something for me in using his influence with the City Hall authorities who controlled the Zoo. I was prepared to swap all my treasures, or most of them at any rate, to secure and save that most desirable young bird.

I must say this for Dad, unenthusiastic as he was about my particular hobby or study, he did intervene and the authorities actually consented to an exchange.

The moment agreement was reached, I remember rushing to

Ballarat Zoo, a mile and a half round Lake Wendouree, for the sands of time were short if not already too far run to resurrect this splendid creature. Sure enough, having got it home, I found it so emaciated and dispirited that all food was refused. I had to employ extreme measures in administering oil, also chopping mice finely and forcing them down its throat besides creating a small, but natural environment as a psychological impetus.

'Ferox', as my mother suggested I call the important arrival, hovered between life and death for a whole week but one night inspired tremendous enthusiasm by seizing a small rat and eating without assistance. This cheering step forward restored my own appetite to its normal hearty proportions.

Much later evidence indicated that Ferox was of male sex, but now the fact that this avian prize had decided to live was all that mattered. He began to develop into a magnificent bird. The snow-white down, golden yellow eyes—one might, in fact, describe those of many older birds more accurately as orange—the powerful build and that inimitable haughty stare attracted me more strongly than ever. By the rarest and most fantastic freak of fortune, we could now actually study a Powerful Owl at close quarters.

Mother, who was an artist of great ability, suggested that she should make a study of Ferox in oils, so after we had arranged a backdrop of gum saplings to disguise any sign of artificial background, she set to work with loving care. That masterpiece hangs above me now. Mother has gone, but her study of the Powerful Owl is unique. Wherever one moves in the room, Ferox's eyes follow: there is no escape.

One year, Mother nominated this painting as her major exhibit at the annual exhibition of the Victorian Women Painters' Association. Believe it or not, the selection committee rejected her striking painting of Ferox as unsuitable. They would not permit his portrait to be hung because anything to do with owls was frightfully unlucky.

So this unique and arresting artistic study, the only one of its kind of such a rare and truly Australian subject, did not appear in the art show amongst the landscapes, flowers, nudes and other odds and ends that appear so often and with such monotonous regularity. The Selection Committee never realized what a loss had been theirs.

From his portrait Ferox looks down upon me now with that unwinking, golden-eyed stare. In it are the dignity, the elusiveness and the mystery that caught us in our boyhood days. For me, he is the intangible spirit of the solitude, charm, cleanliness and scented atmosphere of the unravaged bushland beloved of my mother who now rests quietly herself under the stars overlooking the very Mount Cole from which Ferox hailed.

By early 1927 Ferox had blossomed into almost all of his adult plumage. As later with others of his kind, I found him unusually difficult to please in a captive state, choosy of roosting positions and general surroundings and easily stampeded because of extreme nervousness concerning anything out of the ordinary.

He was rigidly selective in diet, preferring clean 'wholesome' perfectly fresh rats. For the first time in March of the 1927 autumn, in a frosty dawn, we heard him call in the deep, mournful 'whoo-whoo'. It was the most fantastic thrill since that first visit to Korweingeboora forest of three years before.

I looked forward now to a first-class rendering sometime in the near future of the hair-raising screams we had heard so much about.

It was a crucial year in my life for, despite Dad's pessimistic prophecies about time-wasting Natural History, this particular interest proved the moving force behind a recommendation on my behalf to the Education Department of Victoria by W. H. Elwood, Principal of Ballarat Teachers' College. Here, in 1926, by virtue of my junior master's position at the Grammar School, I had perforce to attend lectures and pass examinations to secure a Primary Teacher's Certificate.

Mr Elwood was instrumental in obtaining for me a full Studentship aimed at a Science course (majoring in Zoology and Botany) at Melbourne University, and an eventual Diploma year in education. So in 1927 I became a free place student attached to Melbourne Teachers' College, residing at Ridley Theological College, teaching part-time and attending the University full time as a Science undergraduate. They told me I was destined, at the end of my course, to carry on the work laid down by the late Dr J. A. Leach in Nature Study throughout Victorian State schools.

Perversely 1927 then, to a fellow not really designed by Nature as a student and who shrank from big city life, was equally as black and almost as devoid of hope as the time I began my brief career as a chemist. The living allowance was a pittance, my only conveyance a push bike, and I missed the bush life like a migratory bird with a broken wing at the fall of the year.

The greatest consolation among odd tiger snakes, possums, and a wombat named 'Essie', was my symbol of all that was wonderful and above all my link with the wild—namely Ferox, housed in an aviary built over a pepperina tree outside my study.

Principal Wade of Ridley College, a man of great understanding and sympathy, whose son was my mate and fellow student, kindly allowed me to keep him there for furtherance of Powerful Owl study.

Actually, Ferox, Essie the wombat, and the brilliantly coloured Werribee tiger snakes became cherished College possessions, exhibited to visiting Church dignitaries and students from a variety of assorted faculties. Resident colleagues in Arts, Medicine, Theology and Commerce, spent many of their free hours in the new, exciting and largely recreational pursuit of rats with the result that the tigers and Ferox seldom lacked for the best in rations. Ferox felt so good that, on mellow moonlight nights around ten o'clock and even up to midnight, he indulged in sporadic far-carrying 'whoo-whoos' that reverberated about the quadrangle. At such times an upper floor window would eventually fly up, accompanied by the yell of 'Fleay, can't you keep that bloody owl quiet?' Usually there was the thump of a rubbish basket or football landing on his aviary roof. Habitually, Ferox took sufficient notice of this lack of appreciation on the part of his audience to shut up for perhaps half an hour. Then he would 'woo-hoo' again, causing further window action indicative of various owners' real or simulated annoyance. By morning, after most of the twenty-two rooms had contributed noise suppressors, the roof of Ferox's aviary presented the appearance of a jumble sale with books, hockey sticks, cricket pads, balls and assorted boots.

In the morning everyone gathered up their ammunition again and to their everlasting credit, over the whole of the five years Ferox lived among those wild students, there was never one serious gesture to cause him harm. He had become a College institution and more than my own personal pride and joy.

Perhaps he was also about the only one to maintain his equilibrium in a world of practical jokes because no one ever dared subject him to any real indignity.

Even the College cow was transported up steps and stabled for a day in the study of a temporarily absent Theolog. who returned to read the bold placard 'Abandon Condensed Milk all Ye Who Enter Here!' I think he decided to do just that after settling down with hose and broom to an after-milking routine.

There was the swarm of bees, with firmly established comb, in another man's chest of drawers, flying in and out of a window gap when he returned after a fortnight's absence. The College Chaplain entering his study to the impressive fly-past of 80 sparrows to which he'd unwittingly played host all day—the matrimonial advertising —pictorially aided—on behalf of various innocents in Melbourne's daily papers—the perfectly made beds far up in the College gum tree when one returned late at night—the dear old cow once more investing the place with a Royal Show atmosphere, wearing a race track around the lawn, inside a hitherto spotless marquee erected for the reception of a visiting Bishop of Tanganyika. The crowning glory of a white-handled 'Nightjar' upon its spire and the bold pedigree announcement 'Out of Marquee by Three O'clock' failed to mollify the irate clergy upon that famous day!

Even the initiation revels—one of which in 1929 gained a front page of Melbourne *Truth*—passed annually in disorderly array before Ferox. It was a strange atmosphere indeed for this natural recluse of Australia's hidden gullies in the mountains.

Of all that diverse group of up and coming Ridley fellows, in 1927 I was probably the craziest. I'd been away from school so long that study irked me, but, above everything else, I craved to get back to the bush. The only thing that could possibly be done about this, after scraping together whatever money was available, was to board the Adelaide Express, bicycle included, on a Friday evening, get off at Ballan half way to Ballarat, meet James Neil, now of Geelong Grammar School, or some other cobber, and ride hail, rain or moonshine into the dark hills and the haunts of the Powerful Owl. After all, we hadn't yet found what time of the year they nested, whether they lived in pairs and when or why they uttered the alleged banshee screams. Those strenuous weekends when we lived again like Burke and Wills, existing on poor fare, freezing by night but moving all day, were sheer delight for which I felt all the better, but the pre-daylight rush to return to lectures by 9.00 a.m. Monday took its toll. I slept through many of them, failed to concentrate and at the end of 1927, crashed in almost every subject. By a miracle, the free place I had not deserved was not lost, but held open, and I was jolted into stark awareness that only a slim opportunity remained. It was sink or swim, with chances verging on

Opposite: *Ferox, the first of our Powerful Owls, photographed with a rabbit carcase at Ballarat, Victoria, in 1926. 'He began to develop into a magnificent bird—the snow-white down, the powerful build and that inimitable, haughty stare attracted me more strongly than ever.'*

Ferox, male Powerful Owl, originally from Mt Cole, western Victoria, taught us many things about his exclusive kind.

Male Powerful Owl, Ferox, in his years as an exhibit at Melbourne Zoological Gardens (1934-37), occasionally flew to his feeding block in late afternoon to seize his one rat ration.

Ferox, Powerful Owl male, 1933.

Buckley and Nunn's as they used to say in 'the frozen south'. Scholastic success meant continuity in Natural History but failure spelt entry into some humdrum existence too dreary to contemplate.

This was a serious time in world and Australian affairs, with the depression years almost upon us and it had become obvious to me now that the difficulty of concentration on the study of lifeless things in a laboratory was a chore that had to be faced and overcome.

So I worked hard and made it the following year. I had earned a little money from illustrated natural history articles on Powerful Owl trips in the Ballan forest and on overland cycle trips to Moira Lakes in New South Wales—the grand haunt of tiger snakes on an overflow of the Murray River.

Hence cheques from the Melbourne *Argus* and *Australasian* and their helpful editors enabled me to buy a second-hand Harley-Davidson motor cycle and so for the first time, distance was annihilated. So too, on a number of occasions, did I almost annihilate myself. It now became feasible to sneak in odd visits of investigation, not only to the big owls of Korweingeboora but further afield in eastern and western Victoria. At Mount Cole in the Beaufort district, V. one night, a far and faint 'woof-woof' at the head of a deep gully led me to mimic the bovine sound. With a hand spread over my mouth, I was going merrily ahead with a spaced interval of fifteen seconds between one double call and the next, when a large shadow arrived on high limbs overhead. The Powerful Owl said nothing but from the manner in which it wound its head from side to side, it was obviously debating active dispute with the trespasser in its territory, had he happened to be one of its kind. With Bert Morris I searched high and low, from gully to gully, but failed to find this bird's daylight camp.

The caretaker of Cave Hill Tourist Resort on the other side of the mountain, described a nerve wracking screaming noise ending in a moaning fashion, which he said came at night from directly above his tent in the fern gully. He said it made his blood run cold.

Consequently, for several evenings we kept vigil near his camp, and at about ten o'clock one night in the weak light of those earlier electric torches, saw a fairly large owl indistinctly as it blundered, puzzled by the beam, through the leaves of a eucalypt. However, it failed to utter a single note.

Cardinia Creek Beaconsfield, Graceburn Creek Healesville, and the deep valleys of mountain country in far eastern Victoria, also yielded evidence of Powerful Owl presence, mainly in the shape of nocturnal calling in the usual 'woof-woof' or 'whoo-whoo' calls. We found odd perching spots which were betrayed by the large untidy pellets of fur-wrapped possum and glider bones and characteristic thick creamy whitewash, totally unlike that of any other Australian bird of prey.

Never in these wild bush jaunts—and very remarkable in the light of later knowledge—did we see more than one bird at a time. Also, all efforts to tune in during night camps in the wilderness proved fruitless as far as the screams were concerned.

In 1931, Ferox and I left Ridley College and the University complete with a hard-won Degree in Science and an Education Diploma. I married a fellow student, the former Miss M. S. Collie, B.Sc., and began teaching as a means of livelihood. Ferox maintained his status as almost certainly the first and only suburban Powerful Owl in history. In student days he'd 'woo-hood' under the night skies of Parkville—now it was Auburn on the opposite side of Melbourne. Later again, Studley Park Road in the suburb of Kew became his home.

He was still very much a natural history treasure and a vital part of a plan whereby I hoped some day to breed the species, and gain a wider knowledge of his fascinating kind. However, as we could find no record of any other Powerful Owl then, or ever, prior to this in captivity in any zoological collection in Australia and as we had found no nests, the project was certainly somewhat nebulous.

In those early days, apart from Ferox, we domesticated quolls ('native cats'), wombats, marsupial mice, eagles, hawks, snakes and lizards, watching them at close quarters and recording breeding events of interest, while patiently awaiting a posting to that long-awaited position for which the Education Department had designed my particular training.

Meantime, I took bright-eyed furry creatures to school and fitted in object lessons on native, very much alive, Australian creatures whenever a spare period could be found. At Toorak Central School, where the soon-to-retire headmaster was an office-bound invalid, the school's first assistant, Vincent Kelly and I and the children, founded one of Victoria's most flourishing 'co-operative' societies.

Mr Kelly oozed a contagious enthusiasm for choral music and took half of the senior school for singing whenever, and wherever, possible. On my part, I entertained and was received with great enthusiasm by the remaining boys and girls in periods of Australian bush lore. At this school, we found that the only discipline for misdemeanors was a hint of possible banishment from special sing-songs or coming visits by 'Miss Wenda Wombat', 'Gerry Goanna' or 'Peter Possum'.

Mr Kelly went on with signal success to train Victorian Championship Boys' Choirs, while a year later after transference to a less congenial school, I managed (with some difficulty) to arrange an interview with both the Director and Deputy Director of Education.

'Admirable,' they said. 'A splendid idea to give Victorian children living lessons on their own animals and birds, but anything in that line must not interfere with the curriculum. You will have to work on such projects strictly in your own time, perhaps after school or on Saturday mornings.'

So, in March 1934 with Melbourne's centenary year coming up and Messrs Scott and Black in England weighing their chances, but not knowing how triumphant they would be in that fabulous England-Australia air race, I, too, balanced my prospects. Rather sadly I said goodbye to 'the kids' and gave teaching away to accept a commission with the Royal Zoological and Acclimatization Society of Victoria.

They asked me to design, build and stock along educational lines, a purely Australian section at the Melbourne Zoological Gardens.

The idea was the brain child of Mr Fred Lewis, progressive pioneer chief of Victoria's Fisheries and Game Department. As a Council Member of the Royal Zoological and Acclimatization Society of the state, he was understandably ashamed of the moribund state of the Zoo where the last true enthusiasm died out in the early 1920s with the untimely death of that fine naturalist-director Dudley Le Souef. Opportunity not only knocked, but a world I understood was now wide open at my feet.

And who do you think came to occupy an exclusive aviary at the head of a block of enclosures designed for the housing, breeding and display of Australian birds of the night? Ferox, of course. He showed to advantage as the one and only of his dignified race in any public or private zoological collection of the day.

All-over scope of this Australian section was a mere four and three-quarter acres of rather exposed, inhospitable country on the south-western side of the Zoo.

The depression years were upon us but wonderfully cheerful

men on the dole—normally clerks, students, plumbers, mechanics, painters, carpenters etc., built that zoo within a zoo on limited finance, in record time, under the foremanship of Jim Slater, tough World War I veteran and ex-Lancashire farmer. Never could anyone have secured a more capable, dependable and loyal deputy, and Jim proved countless times his weight in gold in the tireless interest he took, not only in this creation of ours in Melbourne, but years later in another venture a thousand miles to the north.

Alongside Ferox in the Melbourne Zoo years 1934-37 dwelt Boobook Owls, Masked Owls and Barn Owls—all of which we persuaded to nest and of which more anon, but the very success of our section and its public support was its undoing. Most of the Zoo Council members belonged to the same vintage as the elderly Zoo Director, and in August 1937, without warning, I was summoned before a Trust Meeting and dismissed on a charge of insubordination. The fact that I had been commissioned to feed animals as I thought fit, did not signify in the least, and so for such things as a downright refusal to feed horsemeat to Frogmouths, which we'd bred for the first time ever, I got the axe. Mr Lewis was the sole Zoo Council dissenter and in those days there was no Workers' Union to protect employees. However a united Melbourne press took my part and tore the Zoo asunder.

Fortunately for the animals the institution never again fell into the doldrums, mainly due to a take-over by the Government of the state and fortunately also Ferox, protected by a legal clause, 'resigned' at the same time.

For just on twelve years now, as you've almost certainly gathered, my greatest interest in nature had been the quest for a closer knowledge of the Powerful Owl. In a varied experience among native fauna, never has any one species rivalled it for sheer fascination, provided such obstacles to a closer acquaintance, taken me on so many 'will o' the wisp' nocturnal hunts in wild places, or caused such bitter disappointments. Rather than go further afield after leaving the Melbourne Zoological Gardens in 1937, I didn't take much persuading to accept the position as Director of the Badger Creek Sanctuary at Healesville. I went there largely because I knew this picturesque mountainous area, with its deep tree-fern gullies and rushing mountain streams, to be the haunt of *Ninox strenua*—bird of atmosphere and romance.

The new home was 'Piccaninny Cottage' beside a similarly named creek adjoining the reserve and surrounded by a healthy forest of peppermint, swamp, stringybark and candle bark eucalypts with splendid manna gums flourishing along Badger Creek.

In those days it was start from the ground up, with the development of this unknown native fauna reserve under the control then of a kindly and helpful Shire Council. In most cases our building material was split from the brown stringybarks of the bush and our meat, to quite an extent, came from donations of old horses and calves we shot and butchered.

Remarkable to relate, it was the introduction of ninety-five large tiger snakes, caught about Murray River lakes and displayed effectively on an island and milked of venom for antivenene purposes, that first put our sanctuary on its feet.

Local controversy about this turn of events spilled over into Melbourne papers, resulting in an attendance jump into the thousands instead of hundreds weekly. The place went on from strength to strength and, needless to say, even the odd breathing periods were devoted to bigger and better planning. One of the first structures was a large sheltered aviary of bush timber and netting, built along a picturesque creek track amid a grove of silver wattles, and here at long last, Ferox entered the environment beloved of his kind.

It was summertime and therefore his moulting season, so that quiet prevailed with practically no nocturnal 'woo-hooing'. In January 1938, however, his slow, deep, double syllables began to waft across the forest lands and incredibly one evening, faint and far away, there arose what seemed an echo! Excitement fairly sizzled! After all these years another Powerful Owl was almost certainly in correspondence with him. His signals through the night skies of so many places, through so many years, were at long last meeting with success.

Interestingly, the stranger and Ferox observed rules that we found later were fairly fixed—when one performed the other was silent. Within a few nights the visiting owl materialized in the early evening, calling from tall trees in the immediate neighbourhood. Came the astonishing sight in a waxing moon, of this diffident free-flying bird sitting right on top of Ferox's aviary, uttering bleating, muttering notes—flying away at my approach but swooping over again in due course, sometimes uttering a single 'woo!' as it flitted past like a great black shadow.

Next night there were two Powerful Owl visitors—the newer one smaller, and even shier, than its colleague. So great was my excitement in those tireless days, that I could scarcely wait for daylight to fade. I was almost equally as nocturnal as the owls. Ferox, I noted, was now practically silent. In my abysmal ignorance, I assumed that the original large bird that had unbent to the extent of roof-sitting on the odd occasions above Ferox, had 'fallen' for him and was therefore of the opposite sex.

So in pursuance of the original objective there was but one course to follow. We had to capture this visitor. Netting Ferox off in a far section of his aviary, Cecil Milne and I made a huge camouflaged lid of the whole roof front upon which the visitor had been seen to alight. Working on the 'figure-of-four trigger' system with the elongated horizontal member a thick sapling perch and the weight of the door propped upon the figure four's pinnacle, great events pended.

A week passed with much 'conversation' but only one close visit and that a glimpse of a big and splendid shape perched blithely on top of the raised trap door. But the night afterwards a hollow slam reverberated down the gully. In mounting excitement we tore to the aviary to find a glaring, fluttering prisoner incredulous at the abrupt curtailment of its liberty.

Still in our ignorance we restored the aviary to its original state, provided extra perches, walled in more of the roof, the sides and back to afford greater privacy, and allowed Ferox to contact his visitor.

Closely resembling him in size and appearance, the newcomer showed more white about chest and abdomen and was evidently a younger bird.

Obviously, and understandably, captivity was particularly odious to this free roamer of the dense bushlands. Neither the newcomer nor Ferox now uttered a single call and their appetites were poor indeed. There were no signs of active antagonism but each owl perched well away from the other.

Suddenly, a fortnight from the time of the wild bird's inclusion, Ferox exhibited signs of severe indisposition, refused food and deteriorated at an alarming rate. The removal of the new Powerful Owl to another aviary made no difference, and in spite of sustained curative effort, to the everlasting dismay of everyone concerned, Ferox collapsed and died a little over a week from the time of onset of his 'illness'.

It was thought at the time that some endemic disease of his species had been responsible, but a post-mortem at Melbourne

University Veterinary School failed to discover any recognizable symptom of disease or damaging organisms.

The devastating fact remained that Ferox, splendid Powerful Owl of twelve year's residence and our very great pride, had died at the onset of a new and extremely promising era. It seems simple and obvious now, but was not so then, that Ferox, as a deep-voiced male, was actually a focal point of attack by the wild owl—also a male; for as I have learned since at the cost of laborious years endeavouring futilely to breed the species, the territorial sense of Powerful Owls, as far as their own kind is concerned, has possibly no equal among other Australian birds. Ferox probably died of what is commonly called a 'broken heart'.

As time went on and the remaining captive owl adjusted itself with grudging resignation to life in the aviary, it became obvious that the remaining free bird, seen so fleetingly earlier, was actually ever present. Never did it approach the aviary but often as evening light faded it 'woo-hood' in a higher pitch, from near or far; and again at piccaninny daylight said goodbye to the night and presumably to our 'guest'. By degrees I mapped out nearly half a dozen perches regularly used. All were within reasonable distance of the captive and none more than a quarter of a mile away.

One on a horizontal upper bough in a tall silver wattle in a peppermint grove was the most popular, and from it the haughty stare of this orange-eyed, rather narrow-headed owl with the typical hawk profile measured one's every movement.

Assuming now that the two birds must be a mated pair, I reasoned, rashly, that could this outer owl but be captured also and a huge aviary with tons of room and a lofty hollow spout be established in dense timber, then a breeding event was merely a matter of time and correct feeding. By degrees then, the favoured wattle tree was fitted high up with camouflaged netting on all sides of the popular perch, except the approach route via which the 'owner' shot in with a typical talon-clutching jolt, and likewise similarly departed. Before the netting 'door' operating on a lengthy pull string was arranged, it was a sight with its comical aspect to see the tall, regal figure perched so sedately on the wattle bough in a veritable box of criss-cross brown netting.

At break-of-day, Aboriginal Ted Smith and I pulled the ripcord in a clock-work operation of extreme precision. Had it failed there was obviously to be no second chance. As it was we were up and down that wattle like 'yo-yos' and operation *Ninox strenua* ended with this smaller, but extremely vengeful owl, clutching with its steel-pliers grip, being lowered from the perilous swaying heights in the ignominious folds of a chaff bag.

No expense was spared in the construction, now, of the tallest and most roomy enclosure, to date, within easy hearing distance of home—yet enclosed in standing timber and walled thickly by a tea-tree palisade. Dragged in by draughthorse, the nesting hollow was pulled into lofty position with block and tackle. It had a deep rotten wood interior being altogether the last word in interior decoration and comfort for the most diffident of owls.

There the pair of dignified detainees dwelt in beauty and grace—my great hope and my despair for three whole years. They ate royally and looked well, but might just as well have been zombies. Most mornings before dawn, no matter how frosty and cold it might be they indulged, as Powerful Owls do, in a thorough bath in clean water but it was crystal clear they'd never forgive me for curtailing their liberty.

There was little calling, no undertone of conversation, absolutely no sign of interest in the nesting location, no friendliness between them—let alone any courting event—and obviously no nesting success would ever attend such an experiment.

Mind you, I am certain that had we been dealing with any of the other Australian owls, with the possible exception of the *rufous* species *(Ninox rufa)*, success under such conditions would have been merely a matter of persistence and time; but I was learning my lesson that the Powerful Owl is a far, far different bird from any other.

With wild caught adults there were obviously no possibilities of progress whatever, so one evening I netted them both—telling the big fellow, 'You're a better man than I am, Gunga Din,' and watched them flit swiftly into the deeper bush.

I had realized for some time before this inevitable end that it was a case of beginning at the beginning by devoting energies to the discovery of Powerful Owls nesting and endeavouring perhaps to get 'inside' the reserve of individuals by rearing owlets from infancy. But how to bring about this very desirable state of affairs? For a start it meant wandering the mountains and the gullies at all hours of the day and night to determine exactly what went on in the Powerful Owl world within the ten mile range regularly permissable in time available.

Taken through tree fern fronds is this picture of the nesting site of Powerful Owls in a manna gum, Healesville district, Victoria (May 1942). The hole entrance was 75 feet above ground, and the nursery floor 5 feet vertically down inside, at the position, approximately, of bough junction on left.

Chapter Two

Nesting of the Powerful Owl

In February 1941 in an area of rough country untenanted by any other Powerful Owl, I discovered an immature bird evidently newly adrift from parental care. White down still showed on the bird's crown and its voice, heard calling somewhat peevishly and hungrily at night, was still the very shrill and ridiculously-thin trill of a Powerful Owlet.

By dint of much walking by day and night, including many fruitless outings, I kept touch with this owlet from week to week. Later, when it developed a mature voice, the period just before or at break of dawn when it farewelled the night, usually served to mark down the position of its daylight roost. From the comparatively narrow head and even breast barring, this young owl was evidently—and later proved to be—a female.

We gradually became almost 'friendly', for the big bird perched in either gnarled apple box eucalypts, red stringy-barks, silver wattles or native cherries *(Exocarpus)*—allowing me to wander to and fro below its positions with no more ado than the assumption of a stately mien and a somewhat frigid stare. Always, in the typical manner of its species in the south, it perched in an open commanding position—shaded certainly and surrounded by densely-growing timber, but permitting an unobstructed view and an easy escape in several directions. At no time in Victoria did I see a Powerful Owl roost in a thickly-foliaged tree into which it could not fly easily or through which its vision was unduly limited.

With the passing of a few weeks the young Powerful Owl's voice matured. Towards mid-March 1941, its voice had 'broken'

Opposite: *Powerful Owl, Ferox, in repose—portrait in oils by M. Glover Fleay.*

and some evenings I heard it employing the characteristic 'woo-hoo', though its early efforts were somewhat high-pitched and ludicrous, often consisting of a single note. At this time its age, calculated from later experience of rearing such owlets in captivity, was eight months.

Winter came and still the lone owl was in its self-chosen area, the nearest wild pair, possibly its parents, being at least two and a half miles distant. During the latter part of July and through August the bird called very loudly and insistently, being heard just at dusk, during the stillness of night and very often, of course, as dawn commenced to break. On frosty nights I could sometimes hear the bird's voice when a mile away from its location.

On many a bitter early morn I stumbled through the chilly blackness, floundering across slippery, boulder-strewn creeks following the insistent 'woo-hoo'. It was the surest method of keeping track and with me it had long ago become a way of life!

The climax of these incessant vocal efforts was reached on 16 September 1941. When I arrived at a red stringy-bark perching tree on that afternoon it seemed for a moment that my vision was faulty. There were *two* Powerful Owls side by side on the roost—the new one (as determined by later observation) a larger and handsome male bird. From somewhere out of the mysterious depths of the far-reaching ranges he had come in answer to the lady's calls. This was the wedding of the Powerful Owls.

From 16 September onwards, the birds were never far apart, the newcomer most likely being, on account of its light breast plumage, a young bird of similar age to the female. Evidently on account of immaturity and the lateness of the season, the pair made no attempt to nest in 1941. Even in summertime, however, when well in the moult, the bond of affection between the birds manifested itself. I sometimes walked through bush towards evening in the month of December and if the two birds happened to be perched together, I would sit at the butt of a tree perhaps thirty yards away and remain still.

Their awakening generally followed the same procedure, the male straightening up, yawning and stretching down a stout leg and handsomely-barred wing. Then he would affectionately nibble the feathers at the base of the crown of his mate's head. Perhaps he might call, though seldom in the season of moult. Then away he would fly, followed later by the female, with that surprising speed, through thick timber, so typical of the species—noiseless like all

22

owls because of soft muffling plumage and the fuzzy leading edges of flights eliminating whirr.

Sometimes in daylight one or the other held a partly-eaten ring-tailed possum or possum-glider in locked talons, though practically always, as I noted repeatedly, the tail and hindquarters of the victim were draped neatly along the upper part of the bough, thus avoiding the effect of dead weight. The owls ate numbers of little sugar gliders *(Petaurus breviceps)*, for I found their skulls and teeth in disgorged pellets. Once the male bird had a beautiful albino greater possum-glider all day on the perch and ate it next evening. He was no connoisseur of marsupial beauty and I suppose this white fluffy creature had been an easy mark. Its decease was a matter of regret, as I knew where it lived and often watched it by spotlight with delight.

April 1942 found the two birds calling very often and loudly at dusk, during the nights and at dawn. Their appetites increased markedly, evidence of this being furnished by the prolific amounts of thick white excreta splattered over ferns, leaves and bark below perching trees. Not every night at other times of the year did the birds make a kill; evidently not always feeling inclined, or in other words, not being hungry enough to do so. I have noted that captive Powerful Owls fail to feed at all on certain nights, particularly during periods of high wind or heavy rain, and also during warm weather. In contrast with Barking Owls they are comparatively inactive.

By early May the two birds no longer perched in different trees as was often the case before. They forsook the ridge timber of their territory and came down and roosted consistently, day by day, and side by side, in a very restricted area in the floor of a deep gully. In other words they no longer wandered about their particular area, perching here today and in another place tomorrow, but became fixed in one restricted locality.

On account of the long trip involved in reaching the birds, some of it by car and the rest by foot across rough, fern-grown gullies below towering range tops, I was unable to keep an absolutely regular watch. The following diary notes will serve to describe their activities as I saw them over most of the ensuing period of excitement, for, believe it or not, after all those years of disappointment, exhausting effort and nocturnal habit, I felt it in my bones that at long, long, last I was hot on the trail of a nesting event. *10 May 1942*—The two owls perched close together on bough of a

23

manna gum which projected into the cover of a grove of tall silver wattles. Plumage ruffled up. At 4.30 p.m. in daylight male bird called 'woof-woof' loudly a number of times. (Right through to end of May birds' calls could be heard for a mile or more through the bush on still nights.)

14 May—Owls still in same daylight position. Big male bird eating remains of a ring-tail in late afternoon. So used to me that he did not pause in his meal. Tearing of victim and snapping of bones clearly heard. Weather bitterly cold. Now that birds are so stationary the thick, creamy-white excreta (very different from that of hawks and eagles) is so liberally painted over the ground and ferns that the most casual observer could scarcely fail to comment.

16 May—Evening, 10 p.m. Cold still, moonlight. Birds within a few hundred yards of same spot. Heard them calling.

20 May—Birds on a wattle bough in same grove. One holding black possum-glider. Also calling close by after dark.

24 May—In the lofty wattle grove male bird clutching hindquarters of a ring-tail. Birds now converse after dark in a rumbling guttural call—somewhat like low bleating of sheep. In the case of the female the call is higher pitched and peevish.

27 May—Not in usual wattle grove. Just over stream within 150 yards in a mixed growth of silver wattles and swamp gums (*Eucalyptus ovata*). At dusk heard 'woof-woof' of male. Crept close and saw the big fellow stretching his legs and wings. Caressed neck of female. He then flew to a neighbouring tree. Soft, conversational continuous notes maintained between the birds.

30 May—In daylight could not find birds in any of usual perches. At deep dusk heard calls about 150 yards south-west of wattle grove. After dark heard the grating, rumbling conversational calls and saw the male give female hindquarters of what seemed to be a ring-tailed possum. From fresh 'whitewash' and disgorged pellets under a totally new blackwood perch (discovered next day) the birds had spent the day within thirty yards of a tall, broken-topped living manna gum with a large entrance hole some 75 feet up near its top. Had thought for a week or so, because of excreta splashed below it on ferns and dogwood, that this was to be the future home of the pair. Evidently if anything like the Barking Owl the male had been scratching and hollowing out a cavity on the floor of the hollow for several weeks. Nesting tree itself stood only 60 feet from the little stream in the gully floor.

1 June—No longer any doubt about the manna gum being the nesting tree. No sign of either bird in any roosting tree during daylight. At dusk, while still light, male called deep 'woof-woof' from entirely new position to west of the manna gum. Answered by rumbling peevish calls from *within* hollow at top of gum. Hidden beneath tree fern below this gum I watched male fly up to dead limb near hollow and call again. Good deal of scrambling within hollow and then female came out and flew to the limb beside male. He gave her a small shapeless corpse seemingly a plucked kookaburra. Then he flew away swiftly through tree-tops in gathering darkness. Female fed, 'scrabbled' her talons on the limb to clean and sharpen them. Out about half an hour. Eyed me off rather suspiciously. No wonder! Uttered her complaining, grating, sheep-like call a number of times. Then returned to hollow. Obviously her first egg had been laid either that day or on previous night. (Both Barking Owls and Boobooks brood from the moment of laying first egg and may retire to the hollow one or two days before laying occurs.)

3 June—No sound of male bird, though evidently close by. Heard muffled high 'woo-hoo' calls inside hollow at dusk. Discovered later that as a rule male does not answer this signal unless he has some held-over corpse to bring straight to his mate at dusk. Did not see male.

7 June—Male bird had moved out of perch in near-by blackwood at 4.45 p.m. Still very light. Sitting on upper limbs of dead tree just over creek from nest tree. Section of ring-tail in talons. Female did not come out until nearly dark. Silver-grey possum nearby frightened and uttering scolding danger notes. As I sat motionless a bright-eyed Swainson's phascogale (pouched mouse) emerged from a hollow log and ran perkily up and down my trouser leg.

9 June—Male called deeply from 300 yards across creek to north at dusk. Had perched in a red stringy-bark at foot of ridge. Few muffled high-pitched calls from female inside hollow. Did not come out. Nor did male come over with food to encourage her out. At no time, either during incubation or feeding of young, did I see male more than alight at entrance to hollow. He *did not go in at all*. (The nesting hollow itself, as we discovered some weeks later when the tree was climbed, ran vertically downwards for five feet with the entrance in the top side facing north.) In four subsequent cases of nesting Powerful Owls I observed in Victoria, nursery situations have been situated in 'perpendicular' holes from four to six feet below an upper entrance. How these big birds manage the feat of such difficult scrambling is quite extraordinary.

11 June—Very frosty. 'Whitewash' had increased below nesting tree, particularly below one dead bough near 'hollow' entrance where male probably spent a good deal of the night after returning home with his victims. Whitewash also under various trees within a radius of 40 yards. No sign or sound of male. At dusk several high calls of 'woo-hoo' from inside hollow succeeded by peevish grating rumbles. When no response came from male the hen desisted. Did not see her come out.

12 June—Cannot always find male now. Evidently has one or two new positions, but not far away. Tonight at dusk high-pitched 'woo-hoos' (five in all) heard from inside tree. Male called about same time further west on creek fringe. No sight of either owl. Noticed that, dating from early days of incubation, style of 'woo-hoo' uttered by male has altered altogether. They are exceptionally deep, slowly uttered, hushed and deliberate—sometimes only one note at a time.

15 June—Saw male in morning. Sitting in tall wattle grove first mentioned. The bird was wet from a predawn bath in the creek. He had his back to me and was muttering to himself. Below perch, among pellets, lay stomach and intestines of a black possum-glider.

16 June—Weather cold, frosty and foggy. Fruitless uncomfortable trip.

19 June—Windy night. Only one call from outside male owl. No sound from female. Naturally on moonlight nights with the male bringing food home at a later hour I was liable to miss the feeding process. During moonless periods it was noticeable that the hen usually emerged at dusk, being called out by the male, who usually had something for her. On these dark nights he evidently hunted by evening or dawn light.

23 June—Visit at dusk. Still and clear. Male calls from wattle grove. Flies over to dead bough near hollow carrying what might have been a sugar-glider (he had held it all day). Much scrambling as female mounts wall inside hollow. Male unconcernedly fed himself holding corpse under his talons and tearing at it, in spite of having called her out. She flew down to the creek evidently for a drink and returned within four or five minutes. Female finished the meal and returned to hollow after a total absence of some 15 minutes. Activity tonight follows several days of blustering rough weather and rain.

27 June—Today found crumpled and several-weeks-old remains of a soft-shelled egg beneath a favourite dry perching tree just across creek. (However, in three seasons' observations in this district and others elsewhere Powerful Owls, conservative here, as in so many other aspects, never produced more than two eggs to a clutch—a fact borne out in later years by Mervyn Goddard who has inspected the clutches of 12 additional pairs.)

29 June—A dull, wet morning with male perched on side of a ridge spur opposite home site. Huge pellets disgorged showing bones and fur of black possum-glider. Standing haphazardly below observing things in general when he 'whitewashed' me thoroughly—a case of copping the lot!

3 July—Violent cyclonic winds for days. Limbs torn down everywhere. Have wondered how male managed to hunt successfully. At dusk male sitting on dead tree near nesting site bracing himself against howling gusts of wind. Seemed most anxious. No food. No sign of female.

5 July—Bush still wet, dripping and cold. Female owl calling impatiently in hollow before dusk. No sign or sound of male. Evidently after high winds and heavy rain all previous night, had gone early to hunt. Heavy snow tonight. What a time to indulge in a nesting event!

9 July—Still, quiet evening, inclined to rain. Male in tall wattle grove with some small prey in talons. While still well daylight flew straight to nesting tree from inside which female had been calling, not in 'woo-hoos', but in repeated urgent rumbles. When nearly dark she scrambled out and flew to near-by dead tree. Male followed and gave her the corpse in his beak, the two birds being strongly silhouetted against western sky. Female fed rapidly, flew to another dead tree rumbling peevishly, 'scrabbled' her talons and hurried back to her nest still carrying the remains of the food. *This she took down into hollow* for the first time and I heard her uttering entirely new notes—soft caressing sounds, 'wook-wook-wook' etc. Without any doubt youngsters, or one at least, had hatched (and observations I made during other seasons plus the foregoing *place the incubation period fairly reliably*

27

at 38 days—that is, one or two days longer than the time taken by the Barking Owl.) After this I rarely heard the female 'woo-hoo' inside the tree again. She uttered her peevish grating rumble and often 'spoke' in caressing mother tones to her offspring.

11 July—Female rumbling repeatedly inside hollow at dusk, but no sign of male.

12 July—Male perched in a near-by blackwood. No food in talons. Departed at dusk without a call. Wild and windy night. Great dead tree had fallen on spot where I usually sat.

13 July—Male up in tall wattle grove with ring-tail in talons—did not fly to nest at dusk. Moonlight now. Female and owlets probably well supplied. Fox had chewed up some of the disgorged pellets on the ground. He'd be lucky to find nourishment there!

14 July—Frosty. At dark, high urgent 'woo-hoos' from female in hollow. Food position evidently bad. No sign of male. Eventually after scrambling noises female struggled out—flew rapidly a long way up creek. She seemed to miss facilities of the dead tree that had fallen. Quarter hour later female returned still without food (male did all the hunting). She had evidently been out for exercise and a drink. Entered hollow and could be heard 'talking' to the owlets.

15 July—Usual sight of male flying across at dusk with eucalyptus-flavoured hindquarters of ring-tail. Female came up to hollow entrance, saw me, and 'froze' for a time. Flew up creek and male followed with food. Twenty minutes later female returned carrying the ring-tail and endeavoured to take it down hollow. Became temporarily jammed when the tail and claws of the possum stuck at entrance. Notice now that, differing from the incubation period, male bird no longer needs to call female from hollow to receive food. He simply utters the rumbling grating note and out she comes.

17 July—Male up in wattle grove holding what seemed to be a plucked Kookaburra. Female came out before dark. Uttered no calls. Then flew to tree up creek and called 'woo-hoo' for a time. Male flew to her and offered food. Not accepted. She concentrated on sharpening her talons and fluffing her feathers and then passed excreta. Male proceeded to eat prey himself. Female flew

Opposite: *At eight weeks two young female Powerful Owls from McLennan's Creek (SE. Queensland 1964) present a striking spectacle, with orange-yellow eyes, snowy down, yellow toes and polished black talons. Weights 2 lb. 5 oz., 2 lb. 4 oz.*

28

Darker and heavier Victorian Powerful Owlets (Mt Riddell 1942) at eight weeks. The larger male (right) has noticeably more definite markings than the snowier female. Compare these birds with the similarly-aged northerners.

Opposite: *The author with a pair of southern Victorian Powerful Owlets (Mt Riddell, Healesville, Vic.) aged 6½ weeks. Large dark-breasted male on right shoulder, smaller snowy-breasted female, Hookie, on hand.*

almost straight back to hollow where she evidently had food. 'Whitewash' below male's perch very plentiful indeed. With double hunting and cold weather his own appetite is obviously very large.

18 July—No sign of male. Female rumbled gently inside hollow at dusk. Emerged later than usual after lot of scrambling of talons on wood. Carrying a lump of ring-tail skin and fur, which she dropped in the scrub. Flew down to creek for drink.

20 July—Male perched in peppermint below a clump of mistletoe on lower spur of ridge across creek, holding half a ring-tail. At deep dusk female rumbled inside hollow. Male flew over and they met on a dead tree 50 yards from nest. Few soft 'woo-hoos' given and then female entreated male for possum. However, he commenced to feed himself, stretching up in silhouette as he tore the flesh from carcase held against limb by means of his talons. Disappointed the female returned to hollow in which she continued to utter her plaintive grating call.

21 July—Female called inside hollow at deep dusk. Some rumbles and soft conversational notes to youngsters. Owlets themselves not heard, though in their first days thought I could hear some shrill whistles just as Whistling Eaglets may be heard from the ground when first hatched.

22 July—Female rumbled gently inside when just dark. Clawed her way up hollow and flew away without delay. Near me she dropped the clean sternum of a bird, probably that of a Kookaburra. Definitely heard shrill notes from owlets.

23 July—Male in tall wattle grove holding ring-tail carcase, as usual reduced to posterior portion. Tail twisted along limb to support weight as is invariably the case.

24 July—Wet and miserable after a violent wind. Male perched foodless in blackwood perch nearest nesting tree. Departed noiselessly at dusk. Female uttered a single rumbling call. Did not come out; evidently protecting owlets from rain driving into entrance of the hollow.

25 July—Evening clear and frosty. Female came out very silently. No calls. Flew 80 yards to dead tree across creek and indulged in jumps, plumage fluffing and talon sharpening. Then flew further away still. Distant 'woo-hoos' heard. Disturbed Wedge-tailed Eagle in adjoining scrub this afternoon feeding on a fox carcase.

Opposite: *Young Powerful Owls.*

26 July—Female now leaves youngsters for considerable time in evening. Male called in broad daylight (late afternoon) and came over immediately, flying high and carrying ring-tail remains. Sunlight still on trees to west. Landed right in hollow entrance and hung for a few seconds before flying to dead limb close by. Female came out at dusk. Male in meantime fed himself.

27 July—Heard one rumbling call. At dusk saw male fly across sky through tree-tops towards east. In afternoon found one of male's perches in a red stringy-bark about 250 yards west of nest tree. Much excreta on ground and large pellets and feathers of a White-backed Magpie. Nesting period responsible for a wider variety in diet. Mammalian food almost exclusively at other times of year.

28 July—Brilliant full moon. Female scrambled up to hollow entrance at dusk, staying there for 10 minutes. No calls of any kind. Flew swiftly westwards.

30 July—Female came to hollow entrance while still thoroughly daylight. Remained 20 minutes in 'doorway'. Flew to bough in top of a green gum and uttered rumbling calls. No sign of male. First sign of moult (which is a very prolonged process in this species, lasting seven months). As noticed in the pair of captive Powerful Owls in my collection at the corresponding time, the wild birds had begun to shed one or two of the distinctively-barred breast feathers.

31 July—Frosty evening. Female off nest early. Could see some small animal running actively in and out of the hollow before her advent. Proved to be a Swainson's phascogale—probably my little friend of June 7th—in the act of helping itself to meaty scraps from the owlets' supply.

1 August—Female must have come off before my arrival. Appeared to the north on a tree-top at dusk. Apparently had had a bath in the creek. Male arrived and called 'woof-woof' but carried no food. Caressed hen bird's nape and then flew eastward. Late moon now. Pitch dark after dusk. Had nasty fall through rotten log which collapsed 12 feet into creek on way home.

5 August—No sign at all of male or female even when fully dark.

6 August—At dusk male arrived from north. Female came out in response to his 'woo-hoo' calls. She uttered conversational 'woo-woo-woo' notes and peevish rumbles. Owls looked very big and imposing against sky. Moving their heads from side to side in curiosity when I stepped out from under the usual tree fern.

30

9 August—In afternoon saw female perched high in manna gum just across creek from nest, facing the hollow. By excreta she had been out all day. First recorded case of young left to own devices. Now aged about 31 days. At dark female flew to hollow, looked in, flew out again, and finally entered. Male called from westerly direction. Flew up with a ring-tail, which female came out and accepted. Never saw either of birds with a specimen of *Petaurus australis,* the fairly large fluffy glider, of which there were quite a few in the vicinity. Probably good at evasive action!

10 August—Afternoon: 'Rigger' Harry Postlethwaite, of mountain-ash high-climbing fame, wearing steel spurs ascended to hollow with axe and took two beautiful owlets, one month old. Hollow two feet in diameter at base five feet vertically below entrance hole. Heavy pungent odour of ring-tails and possum-gliders on floor wood. Debris of possum fur, possum-glider's long black tail, few bones. Kookaburra feathers, disgorged pellets and odorous excreta. Neither of parents in attendance, though one bird (female?) appeared on a bough about 80 yards away at dusk. Not at all pugnacious like parent Barking Owls. Owlets lowered on a long rope, in a bag. Owlets about size of adult Barking Owls *(N. connivens).* Wing plumage reminiscent of Plymouth Rock fowls (grey and white barring). Snowy-white down on breast, neck and head. Tails the merest of stubs. Eyes very small and palest lemon colour, beaks very prominent. Enormous toe development; toes white, not the yellow of adult, talons not yet well grown. Owlets not pugnacious. They lay in 'frozen' attitudes. Disgorged pellets of fur overnight. Felt sorry for parent birds, but owlets necessary to further study.

17 August—Difference in size of owlets noticeable from first sight. This (as proven later) followed the relative size of sexes. Male larger and female smaller. Also variation in colouring of down (see plates), male darker streaks on breast, abdomen and crown, female much more snowy white. On this date male stood just over 12 inches high and weighed 2 lb. 6 oz., and the female stood 10 inches high and weighed 2 lb. $\frac{3}{4}$ oz. Measurement across a diagonal of the spread toes of male was $5\frac{1}{4}$ inches. Owlets beginning to utter a thin, shrill trilling whistle when hungry, occasionally yawning widely with a wheezing note. Tail stubs now $2\frac{1}{2}$ inches long. (I observed the same difference in size and colour of young owlets in a second family in 1943.)

21 August—Unfortunately wild instinct already strongly developed in young birds. Carefully feeding them on their native diet. Able to flutter a few feet. Talons now shockingly large and sharp. Draw blood even when owlets merely perch momentarily on one's hand.

24 August—Owlets aged six weeks. Now tearing up animal carcases for themselves. Large appetites. Eyes now much larger and more strongly coloured (orange-yellow). Playful when alone. Tails still abbreviated. Able to fly a six-feet stretch on to tables, chairs etc. Disgorge large pellets containing vertebrae, toe and skull fragments enveloped in fur. Christened male 'Wookie' and female 'Hookie'. Parent birds still about nesting vicinity. Moulting obviously now.

31 August—Male owlet now 2 lb. 9½ oz. Tail 5½ inches long. Female owlet 2 lb. 4 oz. and tail 5 inches. Both able to fly fairly well, reaching tops of doors in straight flight from floor. Plumage differences more accentuated. Like all young owls they display playful tendencies (though at a distance) in head winding gymnastics. Male inclined to be more friendly than female. Sometimes sat in evening on ends of children's beds amusing them with various engaging antics. Considering exceptionally nervous temperament of the species, both owlets taken a little too late ever to be truly friendly pets.

9 September—Most probably at the stage now when owlets would be ready to scale wall of hollow to perch with parents. Aged nearly 9 weeks. Fly excellently. Tails six inches long. Weights: male 2 lb. 14 oz.; female 2 lb. 6½ oz. Talons fierce and merciless. Birds a brilliant sight with their snowy down, colourful eyes and upright regal attitudes. Look almost as large as adults in their fluffy plumage. Wings and back lack the strong brown of the adult. More greyish.

14 September—Special large aviary converted for the owlets. Male has developed a remarkable coughing sneeze accompanied by shaking of head. Appetite still excellent.

15-23 September—Condition of male owlet deteriorating with brownish fluid coming from nostrils after coughing. On 23 September sad disappointment of bird's sudden death in midst of a coughing bout. Quantities of brownish fluid from lungs. The hoodoo on Powerful Owls remains.

Dr H. E. Albiston, then Director Veterinary Research Institute, University of Melbourne, gave post-mortem findings on this bird as follows: 'Examination showed both lungs affected with a chronic nodular disease and similar nodules were present on the living membrane of the air sacs of the peritoneal cavity. General appearance of the lesions were strongly reminiscent of those seen in fowls affected with the air-sac mite *(Cytoleichus nudus)*. The nodules are the result of the body defence processes in which the parasites are encapsulated and subsequently degenerate. The contents of the nodules in the owl had completely degenerated, and we were unable to find any structures which could be identified as parts of the bodies of mites, and on which the diagnosis could be definitely established. There was no evidence of a bacterial or mycotic infection, and although proof is lacking I feel fairly confident that *C. nudus,* or possibly a similar form *specific* for *Ninox strenua,* was the cause of the trouble.'

(This was my first experience of this disease in immature Powerful Owls, but in view of later knowledge, I am of the opinion that this trouble of the respiratory system could possibly be one of the reasons for the comparative rarity of the species.)

4 October—Hookie, the remaining young female owl, in excellent fettle. Haughty and dignified. Still very snowy-white on under parts and neck, but several true brown-barred feathers have appeared on neck and on both flanks of abdominal region.

12 December—Hookie now displays a line of V-barred feathers running down each side of undersurface from neck to abdominal flank. Legs feathered and crown partly so. Voice still the shrill piping trill. Rarely used unless I call to her and she is hungry.

31 January 1943—Hookie practically fully feathered though not the dark brown general colour of an adult. She is a light-coloured bird with a good deal of white showing in the brown barring of the undersurface. (Some mature birds darken so much with age that little white is visible on the breast.) Crown still shows some down. Bird nearly seven months old.

12 February—Voice 'breaking'. No longer a clear treble, but deepening.

1 March—Over last week Hookie has made amateurish nocturnal attempts to call 'woo-hoo'. One syllable good, followed, as a rule, by a cracked broken note. By mid-March bird calling very well and could pass for an adult. Usual comparatively-high notes distinguish her voice from that of a male.

General

At odd times at night, particularly in autumn, both in 1943 and 1944, a wild bird of her species came out of the ranges, perched on her aviary and gave call for call. It was a thrilling event as always for one with ornithological leanings to wake at night and hear a conversation between such birds within a matter of yards—but not always an entertainment for others of the household less enthralled with the cries of nocturnal birds!

Undoubtedly with the coming of 1944 Hookie attained maturity and during May and June of that year, approaching two years of age, she displayed her readiness to mate and set up house by sustained and excited nocturnal calling. Several times when a wild bird, possibly one of her own parents, arrived in May, courting notes were heard, but the visitor did not stay.

So much for a sketch of the development of such a bird from the time of hatching.

The next year's brood

At odd times, whenever I could manage to get away, I kept in touch with the free parents in their wild forested haunts, and from the results of several years' close observation on these birds and on yet a second pair located some miles away, I am sure it is most unlikely that the species ever nests more than once in the year, for moulting, as recorded, commences in August with the shedding of small body feathers and is completed only with the replacement of certain large wing and tail feathers during January and February, and even as late as March.

I was fortunate, on 28 May, 1944, while observing the second pair of *N. strenua,* to observe the actual mating performance. The birds were located in a favourite perch on the horizontal boughs of one of a dense and lofty growth of brown stringybarks, *Eucalyptus baxteri*: var *pedicellata,* growing on a spur of the ranges. It was very still and not yet dusk when the male began stretching his legs and wings. He then caressed the neck of the still sleeping female and flew to a neighbouring sloping bough, calling with typical deep-toned 'woof-woof' notes. Soon the hen also awoke, stretched, responded with higher-pitched double calls and flew to the same bough, landing beside and below the male. Then ensued a soft conversational series of 'woo-woo-woo-woo!' notes on the part of the male —the syllables running into one another almost precisely as is the habit of Boobooks. Finally the male stepped on to the female's back and mating took place, accompanied by a soft and somewhat rabbit-like squealing much akin to the noise uttered on similar occasions by the Barking Owl. Both birds flew off to the south-west and the male could be heard later uttering hoarse single notes.

Thus, at last, any lingering doubts about which sex was which, a query that had exercised me considerably over many seasons, were dispelled once and for all. It was strictly from this observation that I could be quite dogmatic in retrospective writing about male and female in the detailed notes on the nesting event.

In 1943, by dint of strenuous tramping and many a cold and damp nocturnal vigil, I managed to trace the nesting activities of Hookie's parents on a second occasion. By this time I had very nearly the outlook of a Powerful Owl myself! Eggs were laid within a week of the 1942 date (6 June, 1943). The tree was a completely-dead, gaunt-limbed, towering giant about a quarter of a mile distant from the previous year's tree, but also close to the creek. The hollow entered fifty-five feet up with a vertical drop of five feet to the floor chamber, and, extraordinary to relate, away up in a lofty crack of the same tree lived a fine black possum-glider. On a number of nights I watched him come out and take off on swift parachute jumps to the surrounding forest. As far as I know, and remarkable as it may seem, the owls *never* molested him.

In due course—with reluctance and a resolve not to interfere with the parents again—I took the young ones. As with the previous year's family, the owlets numbered two—a large, distinctively-marked male and a smaller, snowily-downed female.

Once more I gave the birds every care, applying years of experience in rearing owlets of at least four species, and yet again the dreaded symptoms, apparently caused by air-sac mites in Wookie's case in 1942, manifested themselves. In this case the smaller female developed a chronic cough as soon as she was able to fly. I thought she would die, but three months later, in spite of brownish fluid discharged on many occasions through the nostrils, she threw off the trouble and became a healthy adult. Tragic to relate, however, the fine big male owlet, having reached what one might consider the safe and almost independent age of three and a half months, being older in fact than his previous year's brother when he was stricken, suddenly became ill and collapsed within five days, showing a copious discharge of brownish fluid from nostrils and beak.

Such distressing happenings, together with former difficulties in rearing Ferox in 1927, have convinced me that during immaturity this species is particularly delicate and vulnerable to sickness and its susceptibility to attacks by indigenous parasites, such as the air-sac mites suggested by Dr Albiston, may be responsible for a mortality in the wild state. Another piece of evidence, in this case concerning the death of a wild bird in its first year plumage, came to my notice some years ago in the discovery of the remains of a Powerful Owl below perching trees on the distant side of Mount Riddell, Healesville, Victoria. It seemed more than likely that the bird had died and dropped down before being discovered and chewed to some extent by a wandering scavenger.

Caretaker and camp at Cave Hill Tourist Resort, Mt Cole (Victoria). 'He described a nerve-wracking screaming ending in a moaning fashion . . . coming at night from directly above his tent in the fern gully.'

Type set of eggs (A and B) of Powerful Owl collected by Harry Postlethwaite and the author in the ranges behind Mt Riddell, Healesville, Victoria, 4 June 1945; third on the right is an average fowl's egg for comparison.

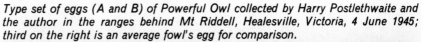

'When I arrived at a red stringy-bark perching tree on that afternoon (16 September 1941) it seemed that my vision was faulty . . . there were two Powerful Owls side by side.' (Female upper, male lower.)

Young Powerful Owl clutching previous night's kill in talons, perched in broad-leafed peppermint, Mt Riddell, Victoria.

Unique study of female Powerful Owl perched in a casuarina tree.

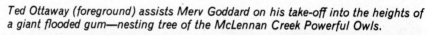

Ted Ottaway (foreground) assists Merv Goddard on his take-off into the heights of a giant flooded gum—nesting tree of the McLennan Creek Powerful Owls.

Giant flooded gum flanked by brush box trees at McLennan's Creek (south-eastern Queensland). Merv Goddard, 100 feet up, may be seen working round to Powerful Owl hollow (far side).

Female Powerful Owl brooding two infertile eggs in hollow of eucalypt, 70 feet from the ground, Kangaroo Creek, Tomalla Tops, Mt Royal Range, N.S.W., 14 June 1959. Photo M. T. Goddard.

'The hen bird flew out (centre in brush box) before he was half-way up.' Female
Powerful Owl watching Merv Goddard at nesting hollow (4 July 1966).

Powerful Owl eggs in situ, *121 feet from ground: aggregate of bones of gliders and possums. (McLeod's Creek, Sandy Hills, via Tenterfield, 21 February 1959.) Photo M. T. Goddard.*

Merv Goddard with remains of four dusky gliders and two ringtailed possums found in Powerful Owl 'nursery', 78 feet high in tallow-wood hollow, 4 July 1966.

Merv Goddard with Powerful Owlets and debris of ringtailed possum and glider tails taken from nest hollow, 4 July 1966 (McLennan's Creek). The larger youngster proved to be a female, the smaller a male—ages here, female 13 days and male 9 days (approx.)

Powerful Owlet, 13 days old and weighing 12 oz., with egg breaker persisting on beak. It was mothered by Scourge and with its brother reared successfully. 'Palpitating throats were a quite normal cooling off system . . . they were extra hot little bods.'

Pair of northern Powerful Owlets aged eight weeks—locality McLennan's Creek, Queensland-N.S.W. border region, 1966. Reared by Scourge. The young male (left) is distinguished from the female by a broader head, heavier beak, and more intense 'pencil' markings on breast.

In the 'short pants' stage. Baby Powerful Owls prior to the flying stage, at 38 days old. Stubby-tailed, plump and snowy-downed, these hen owlets are untameable though taken at the age of 22 and 24 days respectively. Weights 2 lb. 2 oz. apiece— 1 August 1964.

Young female northern Powerful Owl approximately seven weeks old—a most appealing fluffy baby with shockingly sharp, well-developed talons.

A charming but stand-offish baby Powerful Owl. Philip Whiting with the female at nest-leaving stage (seven weeks four days). Owlets taken from McLennan's Creek (4 July 1966).

Scourge and foster child, 22 August 1966. The baby was nine weeks old.

Scourge, hen Powerful Owl at West Burleigh, using her ripping technique on the author's handkerchief. Following such a game a new handkerchief is usually necessary.

Scourge gives the possum-treatment to a handkerchief—holding it beneath her talons and tearing off piece after piece.

Chapter Three

Taking of the First Set
of Powerful Owl Eggs for Science

In our young days and, in fact, right up to 1945, there was only one clutch of alleged Powerful Owl eggs in a natural history institution anywhere in the world.

This belonged to the H. L. White collection—itself a treasure of the National Museum, Melbourne, and was said to have been taken on 23 November 1911 at Kingaroy, Queensland.

The late H. L. White, philanthropist grazier of Belltrees, Scone, New South Wales, described this particular clutch a long time ago in the *Emu,* Vol. 12, p. 21. In actual fact, James Franks, who was supposed to have taken the three eggs, was not a collector for R. H. Archer, from whom H. L. White acquired them, and the set in question came into Archer's possession through the agency of one A. E. L. Bertling. About that time most of the prominent oologists (egg collectors) in Australia were Bertling's victims, and it was not until he was exposed by Mr Frank Howe, who discovered some of his 'frauds', that the egg collectors realized they had been fooled and that the set of *Ninox strenua* and quite a number of sets of several rare Fig Parrots sold by him were questionable. Just imagine the depths to which human rascality may sink when a knowledge of the rarity of natural history treasures is used by unscrupulous 'birds of prey' to dupe the unsuspecting!

There were, however, several other aspects which would appear to throw some doubt upon the authenticity of the Kingaroy set of Powerful Owl eggs. The first is the date on which the set was alleged to have been taken. This is of the utmost importance, in view of the fact that *N. strenua* begins to moult long before November, and that the species is very heavily in moult by the end of that month. Secondly, over a long period of observation and close association with the Powerful Owl, I had, and still have, no evidence of more than two eggs forming a clutch, and though admittedly that is not conclusive, it is nevertheless very significant, even allowing for the reference to what might have been a soft-shelled egg in my diary entry on 27 June, 1943 (*Emu,* Vol. 44, p. 104). Further, the only other evidence available supports the fact that the nesting season for the species is a particularly early one. So there were seeds of considerable doubt about the whole matter, and I often examined those three eggs in the Melbourne Museum, wondering greatly.

Eventually the confusion surrounding the authenticity of the one and only alleged clutch pushed me into a definite course of action. It seemed essential, in the interests of a complete study of this rare and noble species, that an undeniable set of eggs should be obtained and described, thus ending all doubt.

However, as it had taken so many years to become familiar with the wild pair, and as I had taken their young ones on several occasions, it did not seem fair to divulge the actual whereabouts of the old pair to avid observers or collectors. In view of the circumstances, the chief inspector of Fisheries and Game (Victoria), Mr F. Lewis, proved willing for eggs to be taken in order to establish an authentic 'set'. So in 1945 I carried out further observations in the rough and dense habitat between Mount Toole-be-wong and Mount Riddell, in the Healesville district, with the idea of securing eggs at the correct stage and submitting them to my friend, Norman Favaloro, for expert examination and report.

I renewed contact with the orange-eyed, haughty birds on 21 May of that year, and when I encountered them the birds were very close together, the larger male clutching the hindquarters of a ring-tailed possum in one foot. Just at dusk soon after I spotted them, they conversed in deep low notes and uttered rumbling sheep-like calls, so I knew that as in previous years, at this precise period, they were particularly devoted to one another and that laying time was fast approaching. As the days went by, the localized perching of the birds, with associated accumulation of whitewashing excreta on ferns beneath one or two special perches in the vicinity, indicated that the nesting hollow had been selected and must be in the immediate neighbourhood.

Nearly every evening, after a car trip of several miles, I took the rough and trackless trip across ridges and gullies to the particular creek-side where the two Powerful Owls were perching. If the eggs were to be taken it was advisable to get them at as fresh a stage as possible.

On one of these trips, of which there were eleven all told, I was enlightened to the extent of discovering that the Powerful Owl does prey, when the opportunity offers, on the beautiful fluffy glider *(Petaurus australis).* In the fore-running account I mentioned that though the species commonly takes the dusky or greater glider *(Schoinobates volans),* I had not known it to kill members of the very lovely fluffy species. However, on this particular late afternoon one of the birds held the hindquarters and unmistakably thick and bushy tail of an unfortunate fluffy fellow.

On 31 May, it was highly significant that the big male bird was perching alone. Both on this evening and that of the next day (1 June) he called loudly and insistently at dusk on each occasion gripping the usual hindquarters of a partly eaten ring-tail. It was obvious that his mate had laid and begun brooding. On the night of 1 June, he led me to her by flying to a large, slightly-leaning, mountain grey gum *(Eucalyptus goniocalyx)* growing on the side of a steep ridge, some eighty yards uphill, and perching on a lofty bough. High up on the huge rough trunk some seventy-five feet above ground, the lip of a hollow projected slightly, and later, when she flew out of it, the female revealed this as the focal point of interest. Even had the bird failed to indicate the position of the nest, the heavy splashing of thick, creamy whitewash over the ferns and ground below told a tale in itself. This evidence indicated that several overhead boughs had been night perches for some weeks beforehand, when the hollow was under consideration and in preparation by the male, because pellets—usually disgorged in day-time—were quite absent.

By 4 June it was deemed time for the hen bird to have completed her usual clutch of two eggs, between the laying of which there would possibly be at least a three-day interval, if not more. In fact, later discoveries settled this time lag as four days. So on 4 June, the expert climber, Harry Postlethwaite, equipped with axe, spurs and rope belt, accomplished the hazardous and difficult climb to the Powerful Owl nest. The ascent and descent, involving as it did in-numerable unfastenings of the safety belt in order to negotiate intervening boughs and a huge bifurcation of the broad main trunk,

39

occupied more than two hours. Remarkable to relate the female continued to sit until the climber was a mere six feet below the nesting hole. This was all the more amazing considering the initial nature of incubation and the habitual nervousness of these big birds. On flying out she landed with the typical clutching jolt of owls about twenty yards away. There were no signs of attack nor of any aggressiveness at all.

According to the climber, the cavity containing the two eggs on its rotten wood floor ran into the trunk for about twenty inches, with a height of similar measurement, and a width of some eighteen inches. The nesting site in this case was a contrast to the deep hollow trunk entered from a hole five feet vertically above, described in the prior breeding account. Carefully extracting the eggs one by one from the hole in the tree, Harry embedded them in a billy of chaff and lowered them by rope.

It was an interesting moment gazing upon a clutch of eggs which, as Mr Favaloro, Honorary Ornithologist to the National Museum, Melbourne, subsequently confirmed, were definitely the first of their kind ever examined. One was larger than the other but they were small for such a big bird—actually not a great deal larger than those of the Barking Owl *(Ninox connivens)*—and not quite as big as those of the Whistling Eagle, with an approximate weight of 2 oz. Yet the parent birds, which I had watched for a number of years, were fine specimens of their kind. I realized immediately that these eggs were smaller and duller white than the alleged set in the National Museum, Melbourne.

Critically compared, later, with the dinkum set taken on that famous day, the suspicious three in the Museum were found to be much larger, with texture of the shell closely grained and the colour a very pronounced glossy white. Moreover they were inclined to be pointed at the smaller end and appeared more than likely eggs of either the Great European Owl *(Bubo bubo)* or related Horned Owl of America. What confusion this mysterious A. E. L. Bertling must have spread in more countries than one!

There is a happy ending to my story of egg stealing, justified as it undoubtedly was. I lost track of the two adult birds until 15 September. Then I re-discovered them in separate wattle trees about twenty yards apart—the male clutching the remains of a young silver-grey possum. There was a coating of whitewash below several trees in the vicinity and a particularly liberal amount below a dead hollow tree nearby which was about a quarter mile distant from the mountain grey gum where the eggs had been taken in June. Naturally the inference was obvious. The eggs were removed at such an early stage that, in this instance, the birds had not only re-nested but had done so immediately, for, on 5 October two big grey and white owlets were perched in an exposed and almost bare peppermint eucalypt with their parents beside them. It was either their first or second day out, for never have I seen the big birds in such an exposed position. The parents were obviously extremely worried and when I climbed a silver wattle to sit within six feet of the surprised and innocent-looking young, the adults flew off some distance and uttered deep rumbling calls to one another, but again showed not the least inclination to attack. Once the male bird uttered a loud 'woo' caused mainly I think by an aerial attack lodged by a pair of Ravens. The young Powerful Owls, however, refused to budge.

All seemed to go well with the owlets, I am thankful to say, and when I saw them last on 10 December 1945, they were large, sturdy and approaching the period of an independent existence. However, as a student and lover of marsupials, I hated to think of the number of possums and possum-gliders that the parent birds must have collected, as usual, to satisfy those healthy young appetites.

The eggs secured on 4 June 1945 may be described as follows: Almost spherical in appearance and dull white in colour with only a suggestion of gloss. Although the texture of the shell is very fine, the eggs have an area on each end minutely pitted all over. Specimen A has a number of small limy nodules on the large end, two on the small end and six others distributed over the remainder of its surface. There are only four such excrescences on Specimen B.

Measurements in millimetres are: A, 51.1 by 43.4; B, 49.0 by 43.2; and the respective weights: A, 904 grains (2 oz. 29 grains); B, 848 grains (1 oz. 310.5 grains).

An American Great Horned Owl *(Bubo virginianus)* egg I measured proved 56.1 by 47 millimetres—much more in general accord with individuals of the supposed Kingaroy set.

We now know that the Powerful Owl *(N. strenua)* in common with *N. connivens* and *N. boobook* commences brooding as soon as the first egg is laid. In this instance the larger egg A showed 48 hours or more of development when taken, whereas the smaller egg B was perfectly fresh.

Chapter Four

Continued Efforts to Breed
Powerful Owls in Queensland

Official approval in a 1952 move to picturesque sub-tropical Tallebudgera Creek, Burleigh Heads district, Queensland, made it possible to bring in two pairs of Healesville (Victorian) wild-hatched but hand-reared Powerful Owls which were established in specially constructed aviaries with carefully designed loftily situated nesting hollows. I hoped to strive further towards the goal of a successful breeding event and the additional revelations that must go with success.

One of the birds was the female Hookie, now in her tenth year, and a truly fine specimen, while her opposite number was an up-standing male of considerable size and strength.

For years they had shared a large bush enclosure at Badger Creek out from Healesville, but invariably when either of them called excitedly in the courting months of April and May, the arrival from afar of some outside fellow beset by territorial problems would send the inside birds, unable to attack him, 'at one another's throats'. This state of affairs was chronic and apparently incurable.

With a sufficient distance arranged between the enclosures to minimize mutual annoyance among the respective pairs, or any chance of vocal challenge, this new Queensland venture offered fresh and exciting possibilities. But the hoodoo remained and to my great sorrow in that first early spring when the wretched bandicoot tick *(Ixodes holocyclus)* became active, Hookie fell victim to its deadly toxin and ended sadly, though usefully, as a tagged skin in the Queensland Museum.

Regretfully I took her partner to a flying fox camp on the Tomewin Road neighbouring Currumbin Creek, and released him in a land of plenty with best wishes for continued health and prosperity.

Though male and female of the remaining pair maintained a kind of mutual armed neutrality, they looked well, ate well and called well—so well indeed that even though the new reserve is located miles from typical haunts of the species and bounded largely on the river sides by mangrove swamps, there arrived an unwelcome night in May 1953, when a wild Powerful Owl 'woo-hooed' from tall dead spars across the home gully. This episode tore general hopes to shreds for though he stayed a mere two nights and was pin-pointed by pied butcher birds in a daylight perch, of all unlikely places in the middle of dense mangroves, the visit was sufficient to estrange the two aviary birds completely.

Though I persisted for several extra years in attempts to reconcile them, it was plainly another dead-end situation, so eventually it was decided to liberate the owls in the inviting vicinity of Springbrook, where miles of giant timber, wild mountain gullies and plentiful treetop furry folk offered ideal living conditions.

However, they were not released simultaneously—the hen bird being retained for several further seasons—with the idea of allowing a fledgeling male to grow up in her company, and perhaps in that way, if no other, bringing about compatability between male and female.

During this period, on a sunny June morning I well remember playing an old recording of calls of male and female Powerful Owls made twenty years previously in a dark southern gully on a winter's night. When the radiogram switched itself off we were staggered to hear loud persisting 'woo-hoos'!

However, it was no ghost—our lone female Powerful Owl, perched in a distant aviary, was also on the wavelength and, highly excited at those familiar notes in her territory at nesting time, she gave a visiting ornithologist a unique exhibition of the far-carrying double-syllabled cry that the famous John Gould once likened to the voice of an ox.

Come to think of it, never previously nor ever since, have I heard these big birds of the night calling with the sun high in the sky. Those familiar lonely notes sounded very odd in the realistic light of day.

With the newest idea in mind, the finding of a fledgling male was the pressing problem; but eventually in 1964, close to the Queensland-New South Wales border, the home of a pair of the notoriously shy and secretive birds was discovered in a remote, heavily forested area named McLennan's Creek. Remarkable to relate, a second site came to light within a week only twenty-five miles distant, on Accommodation Creek near Wallangarra, Q.

Merv Goddard climbed 101 feet to the first nest in a flooded gum standing in the floor of the gully on 19 July 1964. In the high country it was a cold winter morning with strong winds sweeping the treetops, though calm down below, where we stood craning our necks to follow the climber's movements far aloft.

I have never forgotten the jitters he gave Ted Ottaway and me by hacking tiny finger and toe holds as he clung ropeless, on a three-point system, high on the broad smooth face of that mighty eucalypt, progressing calmly from the trunk junction of one enormous limb to another above, with only that precarious finger and toe clutch between him and violent entry to eternity.

Carefully lowered on a long nylon line, the solemn, suspicious owlets were approximately twenty-four and twenty-one days old respectively and 1 lb. 12 oz. and 1 lb. 4 oz. in weight.

Close by in the enclosed tangle of lillypilly and vines canopying the creek, perched one rather narrow-headed parent bird clutching the headless body of a dusky glider.

On request, Merv also lowered a comprehensive collection of odorous debris from the lofty nursery so that the kinds of prey brought in for the youngsters could be evaluated.

A true-life 'Jack and the Beanstalk' himself, Merv returned to earth reeking of the peculiar, musky, not unattractive odour of dusky glider; for, as you must have gathered by now, this animal is almost always target number one for the Powerful Owl. Here also, with the exception of a tailing-off section in south-western Victoria, habitats of hunter and hunted coincide closely indeed.

We concentrated immediately on the absorbingly interesting task of identifying all the bits and pieces.

Fur from a number of hapless gliders had formed a warm bed for the owlets and the lengthy tails of at least five individuals were intact—not having been carried out and dumped as is so often the case.

There were some skeletal relics of those other gully dwellers, the fluffy (yellow-bellied) gliders—far smarter and not so common as their larger relatives—and traces of ring-tailed possums. No trace existed of the grey-headed flying fox, mainly I should say because of its absence further north during the winter period.

44

'A remarkable character by the name of Scourge—absolutely unique among her kind. For the very first time in all the long, long years a Powerful Owl treated me without reservation as another Powerful Owl.'

An uncommon 'ash-blonde' Dusky Glider. 'Once the male Powerful Owl had a beautiful albino dusky possum-glider all day on the perch—he was no connisseur of marsupial beauty.'

Opposite: Dusky glider—target no. 1 for Powerful Owls—is a common tree marsupial through timbered country of the Dividing Range of Australia's eastern fringe.

Debris removed from Powerful Owl nesting hollow 101 feet high in a giant flooded gum at McLennan's Creek. Tails and limb bones are mostly those of dusky gliders, with remains also of ringtailed possums, fluffy gliders, and portion of a hare skin.

In other years and other places as you will recollect, there have also been magpie, raven and kookaburra feathers. I've never forgotten the maniacal screams of one unfortunate jackass which was carried off into the night within a hundred yards of me by a hunting Powerful Owl under a bright moonlit sky.

The raid took place during a nocturnal reconnaissance of that first nesting pair, so many years before, in Victoria.

Last, but by no means least among victim evidence in the 1964 nest, was portion of a hare skin. So once again one cannot state categorically that Powerful Owls prey exclusively upon creatures that live or perch in the trees. In this case the rodent must have been either immature or portion of an adult, for the lifting of a well grown specimen of greater weight than the hunter itself to the high nesting hollow, would be a matter of insuperable difficulty. There were, of course, plentiful blowfly larvae in the general debris.

The second couple of owlets removed on 25 July from the gum on Accommodation Creek below Mount Norman, north-east of Wallangarra, Queensland, were extremely small, the elder perhaps fifteen days old, and the baby a mere eleven or twelve days.

Actually the prospect of accepting parental responsibility for them filled me with dismay. As yet they were mere pin-feathered balls of down still equipped with egg 'teeth' on their tiny beaks, and so very small that both could fit side by side within a spread hand. In fact the baby was so much an infant and so oblivious of possible danger in the world about it, that it trilled through every waking hour—happily warm in the electric incubator in which both smaller birds grew.

Nevertheless so early indeed does the wild, inflexible outlook of a Powerful Owl manifest itself, that the first owlets and the elder of the Accommodation Creek birds were disappointingly, though scarcely surprisingly, already too far advanced ever to be truly tractable. Yet the tiny helpless baby later to blossom forth into a remarkable character by the name of 'Scourge', was ideal both as regards age and outlook. Just those three or four days of junior status were to make a lifetime of difference.

The rearing of the four owlets took four months out of my life and cost the lives of many hundreds of rats and mice, but all went well and the balls of fluff grew into healthy vigorous birds. Waiting for the ejection of pellets of bone and fur was often an exasperating strain upon one's patience because new food was inadvisable until the mechanism of the young stomachs had completed a cycle of digestion. In other words a definite feeding rhythm was both essential and vital.

Now for the very first time in all the long, long years since I became aware of the species, a Powerful Owl began to treat me without reservation as another Powerful Owl. Unlike her slightly older sister, only a matter of days her senior, Scourge grew up without the usual inhibitions of her kind, gaining her name from a 'playful' habit of alighting upon my back or shoulders and rumbling delightedly as she tried out those dreadful talons and massive beak on this new and intriguing type of 'fur' covering.

When her voice broke and she learned to 'woo-hoo', I regarded it as the highest acclaim I'd ever received when she added this time-honoured signal, in the fading day, in answer to the faintest sound of my voice in the vicinity.

However once again I have gone ahead of events.

I had settled a McLennan's Creek youngster (apparently male) as planned with the adult southern female.

As with most mature hen birds in the breeding season, I assumed that the appeal of an owlet's trilling voice could scarcely fail to awaken her maternal instinct (it happens with other kinds of owls and diurnal birds of prey) and through it an alliance which would lead eventually to successful nesting.

But again I had bargained without the fixed unbending extraordinary cussedness of a Powerful Owl. Although she 'woo-hood' incessantly in early evenings—often during late hours and at dawn with the instinctive urge to make contact with a mate and though she had gone through courting performances time and again about a nesting log, this stubborn lady would have absolutely none of the baby. They never perched together and within a month she had taken to diving directly at the youngster and knocking it roughly off boughs in full flight.

Not only was liberation of the remaining adult in bush towards Springbrook now the sole alternative, but I found also to my dismay that the owlet could no longer be rehabilitated with its kindergarten colleagues. Its trust in both owl and human nature was completely shattered. I paired it off in a large aviary with Scourge's sister bird with the intention of liberation once we were sure that success would attend the main project—to wit the eventual mating of Scourge with the largest and eldest owlet of all four (from McLennan's Creek).

In yet the newest aviary of all, overhung by guava foliage and constructed in a secluded area with special provision of an elevated nesting hollow and natural bathing dish, the owls were over a natural ridge from the others (to obviate sound irritation). These two birds which had never been apart were obviously compatible, contented and vigorous. They were also within easy earshot of my ever-open bedroom window.

The remarkably domesticated Scourge performed frequently with typical high-pitched calling and there was no shadow of doubt about her sex, but her large companion, whom Paul Gallagher, in the interests of alliteration, christened 'Urge', merely rumbled in a deeper tone seemingly acquiescing in all matters and quite content to leave the talking to Scourge.

General attributes and attitude of this bird indicated masculinity in every respect and I knew already, of course, that the female of the species is naturally noisier than the slowly spoken male.

As time went on it became more and more obvious that Scourge was indeed a most fantastic bird given to playful 'landings' upon limbs beside one with a crashing jolt of talon-shod toes shaking the surroundings and stirring one's sympathy for any furry victim unlucky enough to be seized in the wild. Given the opportunity she'd take hat or handkerchief, or anything proffered her, holding it beneath her talons for a methodical stripping down, using the opposing pull of her formidable hooked beak. In the process she rumbled or uttered odd courting notes. It was a game in which she was ever keen to indulge, much to the detriment of the 'playthings' themselves.

So utterly does the orange-eyed bird regard herself as a privileged pal of mine that one day in full sunlight, when I took a brindled bandicoot into the confines of her enclosure for the purposes of easy photography, she awoke and swooped immediately to grab the subject—displaying indignation and reluctance at its hurried rescue.

In mid-winter 1965 with one year up, the birds performed some measure of courtship, nibbling the napes of one another's necks, sitting closely together by night and flying to the nesting box entrance. Uninhibited Scourge rumbled unceasingly and on occasions at the nest uttered continuous 'mor-mor-mor' notes that promised well for maturity the following season.

Eventually the long awaited autumn of 1966 approached, and in mid-March of that year with the moult just about complete, Scourge became vocal to an extreme degree. This busy-body extrovert, absolutely unique among her kind, flew often to the nesting box, particularly in late afternoon, jumping within and making 'mor-mor-mor-mor!' courting conversation the whole time. I think I was supposed to follow her into the hollow! The harsh sheep-like rumbles of an ingratiating conversational type were used by both birds and each evening Scourge 'woo-hooed' softly but consistently from dusk until dark.

Strangely, beyond deep rumbling grating replies and occasionally following Scourge to the hollow, Urge said little indeed, but so friendly, and so well adjusted to one another did they seem that I assumed the very quietness of Urge to be a normal state of affairs—a kind of indulgence to the whimsies of Scourge.

Only in early April did this bird begin to 'woo-hoo' and then, though slow and deliberate, it was a relatively high-pitched note, sometimes double, sometimes single.

I was not particularly happy on the evening of 9 April 1966 to find a visit in progress by a wild Powerful Owl but even the loud calling of this bird from a high dead tree on the river inlet—evidently in response to the dusk and dawn signals of Scourge and Urge—made no damaging impression upon the nesting pair. What a relief that was!

Characteristically towards the end of April and beginning of May, appetites of both birds stepped up considerably and the copious creamy whitewash, typical of an outside nesting site at such a season, splattered the ground in all directions. The owls sat side by side a good deal in daylight hours, with one or the other holding a food item in a clutching foot.

On 8 May, Scourge entered the hollow for the first time and began scraping a depression in the floor debris. She took to perching close by through the days with wing-tips drooping below tail level, and though she never questioned my comings and goings up a ladder leading to the nest, Urge now began to exhibit resentment with bristling crown feathers, raised wings and a fierce glare—altogether an impressive and intimidating front.

Early morning of 20 May brought shock and sudden crystal-clear realization of what, over weeks, had been a dawning, depressing, but ever-rejected suspicion. Urge herself was missing, sitting tucked away in the lofty box. Beneath her lay a single white egg!

Despite size difference, their compatability and behaviour, Scourge and Urge—so carefully nurtured together for almost two years—were not, after all, a true pair of Powerful Owls, but two hen birds.

Obviously the hoodoo of all the long forerunning years clung as strongly as ever. What an extraordinary run of ill fortune had dogged this lifelong venture. Back at Badger Creek I had survived a serious tiger snake bite only to climb the golden stairs—almost for good—following a sixteen foot head-down fall while building a Powerful Owl aviary.

The irrefutable discovery of Scourge and Urge's common sex constituted a heavy blow. Realization of miscalculation, backed by subsequent evidence, indicated that the yardstick of voice-pitch and disparity in size are not nearly so clearly marked in these northern Powerful Owls along the Queensland-New South Wales border region as they are in southern Victoria.

In other words, in observing perching pairs here it is not invariably obvious which is male and which is female, and the voices of many hen Powerful Owls in southern Queensland, though higher in pitch than those of males, are at times not markedly so as in the south.

It seems to me also, though this is not supported by the measurements of Mees, that generally speaking, southern birds are larger and heavier. It is definite that age for age southern nestlings, weighed at corresponding stages to those of northern origin, are 4-5 oz. heavier.

At all events with Urge brooding quietly on the six-inch-thick, rotted wood floor of the nest and coming out only at dusk or dawn, Scourge laid her own first egg beside her on 30 May and the second apparently on 2 June, i.e., with an estimated four-day interval. She now rumbled peevishly—both birds so dedicated to the task in hand that like a couple of broody old fowls neither moved from their side by side position during my visits. Urge bristled fiercely but Scourge permitted any liberty within reason, such as taking her photograph and sneaking a hand beneath her feathers to borrow eggs for inspection. She merely grunted *sotto voce*, treating me casually as her attentive counterpart arriving as I should do at the hollow entrance.

Transposition of eggs was common, but relations between the birds worked to perfection, and in spite of the bitter disappointment, the situation had its compensations.

The final do or die course of action left to us now, of finding a young male and waiting *another* two years for maturity, was one obviously beset with many an 'if' and possible slip. We had, of course, to find a Powerful Owl bush pair, identically situated and in time for transplantation. We must await hatching and finally waft the owlets across a lot of country in the very early days of their lives, before Scourge and Urge gave up the struggle.

So Merv Goddard and I lived again in the border country, reviving familiarity with such picturesque spots as Diehard, Skeleton and Resurrection Creeks—not to mention Wilson's Downfall and Bookookoorara—to check once more on the McLennan's Creek owls. Gratifyingly, the playing of a tape recording brought surprisingly rapid reaction in the shape of retaliatory vocal challenge from the hen owl, seemingly most anxious to discover and intercept the 'interloper'.

Camped on a hillside one particular night in eucalypt, grasstree and sheoke forest, I recall the still and frigid midnight hour when seemingly we shared the mighty forest with the owls, following a strenuous gully scramble deep down below.

How fascinating, as always, that far-carrying 'woo—hoo!' 'woo----hoo!' and again 'woo----hoo!' seeming to sound for miles across the massed foliage of thousands of mighty gums, dark under a twinkling immensity. How peaceful, too, the distant run of water, the warm seats before the friendly glowing fire with mugs of tea, the yarns, the eye-tingling, aromatic smoke, and the endless rounds of butter-soaked toast.

Only a single nervous glider above us broke in on the assertive challenge of the ruler of the forest—uttering abrupt cries of half-shriek, half-chuckling nature.

I drowsed off to sleep that night lulled by the voice of the free-ranging owl, woven as it always has been into my life in general, and which, strange as it may seem for a repeated call, is so unhurried and of such quality as never to savour of monotony.

Traced by Merv Goddard to a gaunt tallow-wood commanding a deep, thickly-brushed, lillypilly gorge from an upper ridge, the nesting hole of 1966 was a spout high above rocky ground.

Judging the incubation time and correlating everything with the sitting birds at home, we journeyed to the tree again to be present on the full moon nights of 3 and 4 July.

At dusk we watched the hen bird flit silently from the hollow to perch in a brushbox and 'woo-hoo' softly with rising inflexion. Down in the jungle of the gorge, the male owl replied in his slow deep voice, but it was the lady who 'spoke' up with vehemence when we reproduced calls from the home birds per tape below the nesting tree.

She was sufficiently disturbed not only to call on and off for hours, but also to tail our progress for a good quarter of a mile. Father owl proved as taciturn as his partner was vocal.

Strewn about the ground below were the remains of at least four assorted ring-tails and gliders, so obviously the feeding of owlets had begun.

Merv made the seventy-eight foot climb at 9 a.m. on 4 July. The hen bird flew out before he was half-way up. From the 'doorway', looking five feet obliquely down inside, he could see two owlets on a floor cavity thirty inches by twenty inches, with an entrance diameter of twelve and a half inches.

Lowered with extreme care, their tender infancy showed in weak trilling voices and tiny downy bodies. Together they fitted easily into a single hand. The elder was approximately thirteen days old and only 12 oz. in weight, with the baby approximately four days younger and weighing a mere 8 oz.

Maintaining hot water bottle heat below blankets in a rubber-cushioned carton, and carefully avoiding rough patches on the roads, I rushed across country that day realizing that every moment counted. Palpitating throats, an upright stance and other evidence of unusual warmth worried me several times on the urgent journey, but it transpired that such indications of heat were quite normal, as seen later under a mother's feather envelopment.

Rapidly growing owlets are extra hot little bods, given regularly to cooling off their systems by this special palpitating type of breathing. In early days it is a very common performance.

That evening I mounted the ladder at Burleigh with some palpitation myself. I removed two of the well addled eggs (one had been broken) leaving the fourth and with it the smaller of the two babies. Both owls had flown from the nest at the time—in fact I had made sure that they did leave. Their startled incredulity as they listened to the shrill trilling of the owlet was a sight to behold but how those respective maternal instincts began to blossom! The timing was perfect because both birds had sat just over a full incubation period.

They listened, stood bolt upright and rumbled in grating tones of anxiety. Within a quarter of an hour Scourge flew in past me on the ladder and, with much head winding and tender nibbling of the baby, settled down to mother it. Nevertheless I kept the second baby away overnight in case of disagreement and possible 'cannibalism'.

Inspection at first light in the morning revealed a warm, settled, contented state of affairs with both 'mothers' happily fluffed and obviously wrapped in the owlet.

Without delay I slipped the second one beneath them also. That too was quickly assured of its welcome and with the remaining addled egg now a surplus quantity—in fact somewhat dangerous—it was removed and 'detonated'.

Motherhood flared in its first powerful awakening. Even the stand-offish Urge refused to be frightened from the nest. I found that extreme caution and deliberate movements, plus a heavy gauntlet, were essentials in any attempt to examine the owlets, for though to my delight Scourge continued to welcome me as her visiting mate, Urge turned belligerently possessive and strikes from her mighty talons not only posed a considerable threat to me, but could mistakenly and promptly have destroyed one or both of the babies.

Though, unfortunately, these involved proceedings by no means constituted a successful breeding event with Powerful Owls, the very trust of amazing Scourge and all the events in time fitted so well that from the point of view of observations it was close indeed to the real thing.

As the days went by, some delightfully intimate habits revealed themselves. Though early efforts were concentrated on the continual covering of the hot little birds, the 'mothers' raised themselves towards evening and at various times during the night. Then I could watch Scourge holding rats (personally supplied) beneath her talons and tearing off neat and tender slivers.

Exactly as had been demonstrated to me under similar circumstances over the years by foster mother Horatia, the wedge-tailed eagle, these limp items were positively dripping with saliva. Scourge woke the owlets and stimulated their appetites for food by repeated 'offering' calls of 'oo-oo-oo-oo'. Actually the sounds were more a series of grunts. Once more the saliva-production is a reminder of its essential nature in aiding the breakdown of flesh protein and explains why it is that so very often when people endeavour to rear immature birds of prey, the little fellows suffer early from alimentary malfunction, contract a chronic ricketty condition and eventually die in misery.

Opposite: *Bristling in anger, a female Powerful Owl presents an impressive sight with glaring orange eyes, bristled crown, raised wings and the ready menace of sharp, incredibly strong talons.*

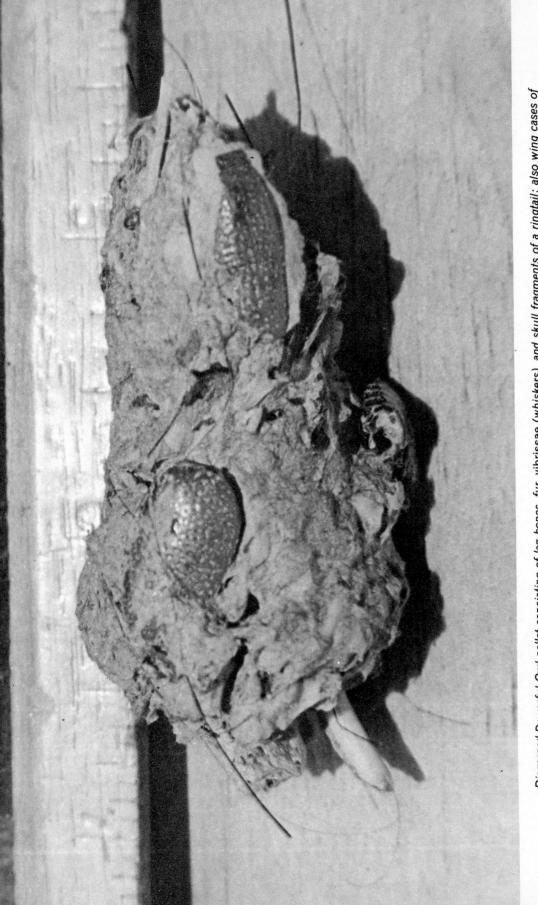

Disgorged Powerful Owl pellet consisting of leg bones, fur, vibrissae (whiskers), and skull fragments of a ringtail; also wing cases of longicorn beetles.

Most copious in the early days of life, the flow of saliva becomes less and apparently tapers off by the time the owlets have attained an age of four weeks. Similarly, in tearing up rats and mice, in early stages only tender fleshy items were selected for the owlets—bones and roughage being swallowed by the 'mothers'.

At dusk and early dark after some days of continual sitting, one or both owls began coming off briefly for a considerable defaecation and an attempt to flutter and preen plumage. No baths were taken in these early weeks.

The sixth night following introduction of the owlets is forever embedded in my memory because I might never have been able to watch another sunrise. It was early on a Sunday evening, overcast and still, when my flashlight failed and I could not see a thing as I entered the aviary to place fresh rats on the feeding block.

Half-way there, moving steadily, I was jarred to a complete standstill by a frightful blow on the head. It seemed as if the roof had fallen, crumpling my hat flat and knocking me sideways. Within seconds blood covered both the right side of my face and my ear (which was punctured) running down to soak my collar and shirt. As soon as realization struck home and the stunning effect began to clear, I dropped those rats and fled the spot at the double.

Urge, the unusually large belligerent one to whom I had always been more or less unacceptable, had deliberately attacked from a height and only by the Grace of God and sheer luck was my right eye still in its socket.

Eight mighty talons, with powerful toes—spear-pointing $3\frac{1}{2}$ lb. of steel-muscled hunting bird—had missed that good old eye, which long ago had survived a grab by a White Goshawk by a mere inch. I was lacerated, sore and bruised for the week that followed. Actually it could easily have been a frontal attack involving both eyes, with the most serious consequences. In that lucky escape I came to realize as never before the power of the onslaught that so regularly catches unfortunate possums and gliders unawares, and so quickly deprives them of life. Never again for me was there to be a Sunday night, or for that matter any other night, when a faulty electric torch could land me in such a simple yet catastrophic situation.

Needless to say, the following day intractable Urge was banished to a distant aviary. I did want to retain my eyesight at least long enough to watch those owlets develop and provide the long-looked-for cock bird. With Urge remaining on the scene I was obviously a coming candidate for the Blind Institute, if not some place of even more permanent pigeon-holing. So Scourge and I (Scourge in particular) remained to rear the owlets between us.

As the weeks went by the baby of the two, roughly four days junior to its sibling, began to overhaul its mate both in size and weight. Equalization arrived or was attained on 22 July when the little fellows weighed 1 lb. 15 oz. apiece.

It was a most significant date, for, from this stage onwards, Scourge left the babies to their own devices in daytime, getting back to outside perching. Their ages, then, were approximately thirty-one days and twenty-five or twenty-six days. They were quite big and noticeably snowy, but differed in plumage in that the younger, bigger, stronger-beaked and later proven male bird exhibited darker markings on chest and abdomen. I would like to emphasize again here that plumage variation and size difference in the sexes in young, as well as mature northern birds, are comparatively slight compared with the larger and more plentifully marked youngsters of the south.

Being reared by a 'mother' of their own kind, the wild instinct, as expected, flourished in these owlets but was tempered by my constant appearances and handling for the purposes of photography, growth, weights etc. Obviously neither of them would ever be another Scourge. They helped themselves to odd food items in the hollow from the age of a month onwards, but Scourge still carried out the main food apportioning.

The older bird was right out of the hollow for the first time at roughly fifty-three days, and the younger (on the same basis of calculation) at an equal age four days later. Scourge sat protectively with them. At this stage the unfed weight of the older female was 2 lb. 5 oz., while the sturdier, heavier-beaked male scaled 2 lb. 8 oz.

With nest departure appetites slackened off considerably, weights dropped by a good 4 oz., and from heavy baby fat with flabby limbs, the youngsters within days developed quickly in wing power and general wiriness. For nearly a week neither youngster seemed interested in food, and production of whitewash ceased almost entirely. However, this seemed quite a normal state of affairs and Scourge didn't worry in the slightest. I noticed now that Scourge's grating rumbles, designed to draw my attention to the need for food supplies, conveyed urgency at times by a raised, ululating, flutey, almost nasal kind of inflexion. It carried further and was certainly given as an encouragement towards greater effort on my part. Additionally a planing sea eagle or an approaching dog brought instinctive high pitched but gentle alarm notes of 'coo! coo!'. At all events, once out for a week, the owlets found their appetites and began to eat eagerly once more.

There were streams of whitewash and their weights (when with increasing difficulty I could persuade them to perch on the scales) began to get back towards those of the nest leaving stage.

By mid-September, the larger young male (twelve weeks) appeared equal in height, though not in breadth, to Scourge. She, on her part, continued to tear up food and feed them intermittently, even though they sought their own, right up to an almost fully feathered but still shrill-voiced stage early in 1967.

Adult feathering began its appearance at the age of four months as two dark lines, one on each side of the upper chest, and co-incidentally with increasing regularity the young birds began characteristic pre-dawn bathing.

Spread of breast feathering was gradual, and the final loss of down and adoption of complete adult plumage occurred as the edges of the crown of the head cleared at the age of seven and a half months.

At seven months there were first signs of the shrill infant voice of the smaller bird beginning to break, or crack, and this change-over attained completion a month later; then over a further period of two months, she indulged in occasional high-pitched, single-note calling by night before becoming proficient in the deliberate double syllables. Now the forecast as to her sex became proven fact.

On the other hand the male youngster, though larger, proved a good deal slower in all-round development. Remarkably enough his voice still existed as a shrill trill a good six weeks after his sister's notes had begun to deepen.

In the early nights of May 1967, forty-three years after the early Ballan forest excursions in the cold and wet of long ago, and forty-one years from first days with Ferox, I heard his first tentative but undoubted deep and unmistakable male 'woof-woofs'. The familiar sound of a lifetime, and indeed the voice of Ferox rose again via this new and callow youngster.

The time was overdue but all clear now for a christening so he became 'Mac' in honour of the impressive, fragrant home gully whence he came.

Coincidentally Scourge was hollowing out a new nesting spot

in the dried out debris of last season's nursery, but Mac was obviously too youthful to take such proceedings seriously.

Not so, however, the young female—his sister—who began flying to the nest hollow on most occasions when Scourge uttered courting notes therein. The intruder usually entered and rummaged about until soft squealing and her abrupt departure signalled Scourge's displeasure at another woman's efforts to interfere in the running of her house.

Now the two handsome young birds were still well disposed towards one another and obviously remained in Scourge's good books but obviously trouble lay just over the horizon. I didn't fancy moving either hen bird because with Powerful Owls, as we know to our cost, such a step is irrevocable and usually the birds must pair off according to inclinations of their own. Long ago I had learned the futility of dictating to such birds as these.

Nevertheless some action would be necessary here quite soon because the situation had a delicate balance. How long before a territorial sense developed in one or both of the young birds? Would Scourge turn on her foster daughter and, in so doing, inadvertently include Mac for ever-more among the ungodly? You see Scourge regards me as a Powerful Owl—wherefore her future attitude to the youngsters was quite unpredictable.

She laid her 1967 eggs on 21 and 25 May respectively, rumbling peevishly about the wretchedness of such performances and in due course settled to serious brooding.

With the onset of this dedicated task the foster daughter entered the hollow unchallenged during the nights on a number of occasions, but Mac was never seen beyond the entrance, gazing in as a gentleman Powerful Owl should do.

Obviously intrigued by the eggs, the young female experimented with them during Scourge's rare off-duty spells, and of course few such brittle objects are designed to stand unscathed against the steel talons and bone-breaking beak of a misguided Powerful Owl—however well meaning.

On the morning of 1 June I found an uncomfortable Scourge sticky from egg yolk matting her breast feathers while shell fragments lay in the rubble about her. At the time I substituted a china egg, adding a second one some days later when egg no. 2 also succumbed to the curiosity of the immature hen owl.

Scourge failed to comprehend such moves and counter-moves, sitting as seriously as ever, but now having considered the problem from every conceivable angle it seemed to me that only one course of action remained, without any workable alternative. Very quietly the young hen was netted and removed to an enclosure completely beyond sight and hearing of the home site.

Scourge and Mac (26 June 1967) now enjoyed a wise and balanced state of affairs—Scourge to sit out a full brooding period on artificial eggs and Mac responding as day fades with hushed deep 'woof-woofs', the male all's well to a sitting partner.

Occasionally he sat right at the 'nursery' doorway doing no more than lend companionship—again the proper thing to do. Often by day he 'camped' nearby with a rat carcase drooping from a talon clutch; and most significant act of all, in predawn darkness one morning (4.30 a.m.) I actually saw the immature year-old male tearing up one such delicacy and feeding it piece by piece to his perfectly acquiescent foster-mother! On disturbance he beak-snapped warningly.

It had seemed good practice in such ways to tie male and female of this true pair firmly together, but I wondered what the future held. Would next season find the hoodoo breaking of its own accord, or was I destined never to succeed in the greatest challenge of my natural history days? Indeed 1968 was the year of destiny.

On the early morning of July 13 that winter, I heard for the first time the unmistakable trilling of a newly hatched owlet. It was being answered by comforting talk from Scourge—ever the epitomy of maternal solicitude. Imagine the impact!!

Here was the first Powerful Owl ever bred in captivity, the culmination of 42 years dogged by unnumbered misfortunes.

Only one owlet hatched, proving later to be of female sex, which did not prevent her being christened 'Ferox II'. In the winter of 1969 Scourge and Mac were successful for a second time— and yet again at a corresponding period in 1970, though in each of these successive nestings, as in the first, only a single youngster developed, despite the incubation in each instance of two fertile eggs.

Both the first offspring (Ferox II) and the third proved females—as nervous and stand-offish as any youngsters hatched in the wild. At a suitable time and age each was liberated in rain forest gullies of the Springbrook range. However the 1969 owlet proved a sturdy male and early on he was set up with a most tractable young female from the tangled gorge of Wellington Rock Creek. It was a foregone conclusion of course that these two should become the 'Duke' and 'Duchess' of Wellington.

Chapter Five

Powerful Owl —
a Summary of Points

What manner of bird, then, is the Powerful Owl? It is far more specialized, less adaptable and psychologically far removed from its smaller but similar appearing Barking Owl relative *N. connivens*.

In spite of its size and strength, enabling it to fly with ease carrying ring-tailed possums and large possum-gliders, it is highly nervous, exceptionally shy and wary, comparatively inactive and normally makes no attempt to repel ascents by man to its nesting site. Swift and immediate flight, caused by sudden sounds such as the crack of falling timbers, is apparently an instinctive escape reaction in a dense environment where collapsing trees and tumbling limbs pose an ever-present problem.

In the Victorian area there is a decided difference in size between the sexes and up to half a pound difference in weight. Such sexual disparity is not nearly so generally marked in the Queensland-New South Wales border region where in the field it is often difficult to tell male from female.

Remarkable to relate, it is the male that is the larger bird, just as in the case of *N. connivens* and *N. rufa*. None of these species conforms to the general rule prevailing among owls and hawks that the hen bird is the larger. In addition to bigger size the male *N. strenua*, in life, is a broader-headed more handsomely-plumaged bird, with a recognizably deeper, more deliberate call than that of the female.

On an average, Victorian male birds weighed 3 lb. 11 oz. and females 3 lb. 3 oz. and there seems little doubt that Victorian birds, in general, are larger than their relations a thousand miles to the north. Yet Merv Goddard (Tenterfield) reports a pair at Tea Tree

Creek, Drake, New South Wales in which the big, darkly plumaged male bird appears 'twice the size of the female' and Eric Zillmann of Gin Gin, Queensland, is convinced that Powerful Owls seen there are 'considerably larger' than those dwelling here at the Burleigh Fauna Reserve, Queensland.

I cannot say, however, that a pair we found in daylight on St Agnes Creek, also in the Gin Gin area, differed in any way from those of the Queensland-New South Wales border areas.

Austere in its upstanding, dignified bearing, this stoutly-built, orange-eyed bird of the night is at the one time elusive and rare, yet a conspicuous and imposing figure, once one has laboriously worked out the round of its haunts from the labyrinth of tortuous, scrub-choked gullies and the steep spurs of its heavily-forested environment. For the Powerful Owl, unless disturbed by bushfires, is a bird of fixed and regular habits, strongly adapted to its life in the ranges, but shunning any other surroundings than those peculiarly its own. One found in recent years perched in the Botanical Gardens, Melbourne, was probably an escapee from the Zoological Park.

Neither bird seeks daylight shelter in hollow trees unless, of course, the female is brooding or nursing small youngsters. Habitually the owls 'camp' on regular perches in a well-defined round of roosting trees in the particular occupied territory. In the case of one pair of Powerful Owls, it took me eighteen months to discover the dozen or more places where the birds habitually slept, but after that I could almost invariably run them to earth on most days of the week.

It is a strong custom of the species, more rigidly adhered to than in any other kind of owl I have known, to take a Spartan bath in cold creek water in the chilly period before dawn.

The Powerful Owl subsists almost solely on arboreal native mammals, including flying foxes in New South Wales and Queensland but rarely bothering, except in the nesting season, about bandicoots, rabbits or birds. However, kookaburras, occasional magpies and even the odd raven or bush ranging hare are considered legitimate game. On only two occasions have I discovered remains of silver-grey possums (*Trichosurus vulpecula*) in disgorged pellets—these being those of smallish younger animals. Victims die a sudden death once the four great toes, two opposable to two, with their lengthy curved talons, clutch in a steely grip. It is worthy of notice that both the native allied and eastern swamp

59

rats, and also the exotic black and Norwegian rats, are favourite items when supplied to the birds. Kittens of cats gone bush are eaten with appreciation by sturdy Powerful Owls, so that here perhaps would be some sort of check on feral cats in heavily forested areas. Ingrained instinct dictates that victims be dismembered up in trees and not on the ground. With security in the food sense temporarily won, the large birds may sit motionless for many hours gripping a pendulous carcase in a locked foot.

Stomach contents of a large adult Powerful Owl accidentally killed in February 1950 in the Healesville, Victoria, district, and presented by me to the National Museum of Victoria, contained not only fur and bones of a greater glider and the 'hand' of a juvenile ring-tail possum, but remains of both a longicorn beetle (*coptocercus* sp.) and a scarab (*semanopterus* sp.). So you see the great possum hunter is not above a flutter among the insects to supplement his diet.

Thick creamy whitewash of Powerful Owl excreta is characteristic of the species and distinct from that of other large owls. It may have its origin in digestion of lighter skeletal material, for bones in pellets from larger gliders consist usually of main limb, vertebral and cranial material.

Two birds of a pair do not consistently camp together, but are usually within calling distance. On calm evenings, and more particularly in frosty weather, the deliberate 'woo-hoo' cries are uttered as daylight fades, even as early as 4 p.m., and just before the bird or birds abandon the daylight roost. Conversely farewell to the night comes in crack-of-dawn calls from the home locality.

From a careful mapping-out of a considerable area of range country, I have come to the conclusion that a pair of these large owls controls (against others of its kind) a suitable habitat territory containing a sufficiency of tree-dwelling marsupials, at the very least two miles square, and usually much more in extent—a lot depending naturally on the conformation of the country and its natural barriers of ridge and valley. No infringement of such bushland by others of their kind is tolerated, the home country being jealously guarded. There is no better example of territorial right.

Merv Goddard's closest distance between resident pairs in northeastern New South Wales is two air miles, and in two other cases three miles and three and three-quarter miles respectively. Often it is up to six miles between pairs.

Belonging to the dense gullies of a timbered mountainous

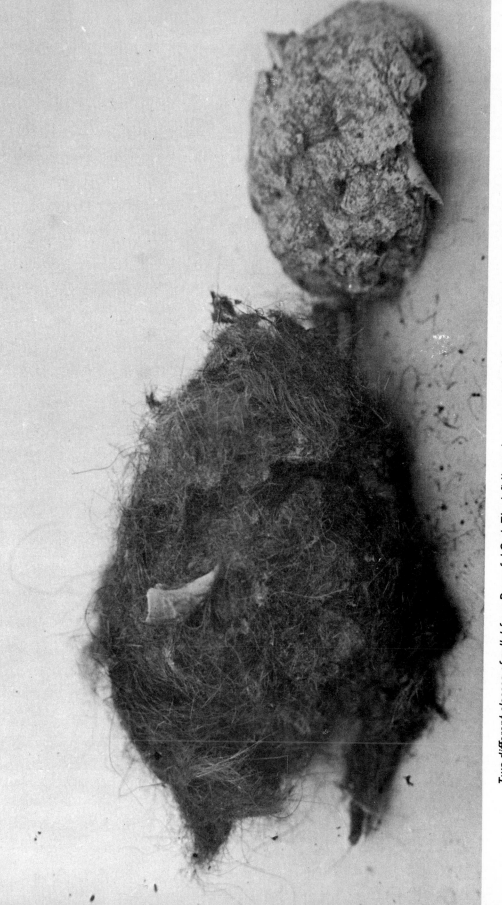

Two different classes of pellet from Powerful Owl. The left (larger) one consists of fur-wrapped bones and claw sheath of a dusky glider, while the smaller pellet contains remains of sugar gliders.

Scourge, the Powerful Owl, nursing owlets thirteen and nine days old respectively
—West Burleigh, Q., 6 July 1966.

Owlets thirteen days and nine days old respectively (left), closely guarded by efficient Scourge, the hen Powerful Owl.

Scourge flies anxiously to the ground when her foster children are removed from the nest for a photograph. The near owlet was thirty-eight days old.

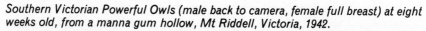

Southern Victorian Powerful Owls (male back to camera, female full breast) at eight weeks old, from a manna gum hollow, Mt Riddell, Victoria, 1942.

habitat along the eastern and south-eastern Australian fringe from Rockhampton, Queensland, as far south as the Victorian-South Australian border but not extending to Tasmania, it is understandable that the ways of this uncommon nocturnal bird should be shrouded in a good deal of mystery. For so many years we have believed its most notable feature to be the series of terrifying nocturnal screeches causing the lonely wayfarer to quake in his shoes.

Yet now after years of watching the birds almost daily in the bush, observing their hunting, wandering through their gully haunts from Croagingalong (eastern Victoria) to Mt Cole (western Victoria), and through Queensland and northern New South Wales bush at all hours of the night, and listening to the voices of captive birds of both sexes over a period of forty-three years, I have absolutely no first-hand evidence that the Powerful Owl is capable of screeching or screaming at all. Whether under exceptional circumstances *Ninox strenua* does utter a hideous yell may be left an open question, but after a most thorough investigation of the subject the evidence is nil.

At our former Victorian home (Badger Creek) we suffered many an interruption to sound sleep when visiting Powerful Owls called in answer to their aviary acquaintances, sometimes perching in a eucalypt over the roof. Always, however, these 'conversations' were conducted in varied pitches of the far-carrying, deliberate and rather mournful 'woo-hoo' or 'woof-woof' notes, with an interval of perhaps ten to fifteen seconds between the completion of one double-syllabled call and the beginning of the next. These are almost certainly the notes that John Gould compared to the voice of an ox and the double sound is uttered with the beak closed. Sometimes the call is merely a single syllable. It might be truthfully said that the 'woo-hoo' of the Powerful Owl by night is just as much a characteristic and distinctive sound of the ranges as the 'quolp! quolp!' and whistling of its colleague, the Lyrebird, is by day.

Careful consideration has brought it home to me that, in general, the female Powerful Owl's double note is not only higher-pitched but shorter in duration. It is more of a rising 'woo-hoo', whereas the call of the male, particularly in southern areas, is a deep deliberate 'woof-woof'. Both birds, however, according to proximity with one another, employ a variety of cadences which at a distance are often liable to confuse the listener. There is little doubt however that the female Powerful Owl is much the more talkative of the two.

Should one bird intrude upon another's possum feeding operation, the resulting sounds of protest consist of uneven, squealing, yodelling notes conveying most obvious displeasure. Arguments are therefore unmistakable.

It is interesting to record that in Victoria, at least, our largest owl is one of the earliest, if not the earliest, bird to set up house. I have known *N. strenua* well settled to the process of incubation while Lyrebirds were just constructing nests in the surrounding bush; and, incidentally, although I've heard cock Lyrebirds imitating such nocturnal cries as those of the possum-glider's shriek, a possum's throaty gurgle and the Boobook's 'mopoke', I have *never* heard them reproduce the 'woo-hoo' of the Powerful Owl, though it is, more than any other sound, an integral part of the *Menura* environment.

Extreme heat in north wind summer days of southern Victoria may bring roosting Powerful Owls to perches nearer the ground— the birds reacting also with loosely held wings and rapidly pulsating throats.

It is interesting to list some of the eucalypts—mostly ancient part-hollow giants of their kind—favoured by the Powerful Owl as nesting trees.

The tall flooded or rose gum *(E. grandis)* standing as it does at gully bottoms often adjacent to, or in, thick scrubs is a prime favourite in northern New South Wales and southern Queensland.

I found manna gums and mountain grey gums used in the south, while Merv Goddard lists also the spotted gum, blackbutt, tallow-wood, white stringybark and brown eucalypt.

The smallest entrance hole measured by this authority was $6\frac{1}{2}$ by 5 inches in a brown eucalypt, and the largest 30 inches by 18 inches in a spotted gum.

Nesting cavities themselves vary from the usual spacious roominess to a fairly tight fit and may be entered from a hole vertically above to one on a horizontal plane, i.e. a straight walk-in.

Closest nesting site to the ground (again from Merv Goddard) was forty-eight feet in a brown eucalypt, Tenterfield district, New South Wales and the most lofty on record, 121 feet in a colossal flooded gum standing in a gully bottom in forest adjacent to brush beside a tributary stream of the Clarence River between Tenterfield and Casino, New South Wales.

In nesting activities *N. strenua* is three months ahead of *N. boobook* and practically two months ahead of the Barking Owl *(N. connivens)*. It broods during the most bitter wet and doleful weeks of the year when southern bushland is at its worst. Courting behaviour begins in earnest in late April and early May and eggs are laid during the last two weeks of May or earliest days of June.

Actually a comparison of nesting times from my notes made in Victoria and those of Merv Goddard collated in north-eastern New South Wales, show that the northern birds may lay the first egg of the season up to three weeks in advance of Victorian birds.

Powerful Owls are in their second season and almost two years old before reaching the state of maturity necessary for reproduction.

Nesting in times of normal food supply is an annual event of the greatest precision and rhythm—first egg of any given pair appearing almost to the day each year—an entirely different state of affairs from that prevailing in the Masked Owl *(Tyto)* group.

Time lapse between the laying of the two eggs fits the later development gap in the youngsters and this year (1967) thanks to the co-operation of Scourge, the 'domesticated' female Powerful Owl appearance pattern was determined with some exactitude as follows:

21 May—First egg laid approximately 8 p.m.

25 May—Second egg laid approximately 7 p.m. giving an interval of ninety-five hours or four days between first and second.

Pairing of male and female Powerful Owls is far from a casual affair and from long experience it is obvious that not just any male and female become attached to one another. Evidence in 'occupied' territory where one of a couple is eliminated by accident or sickness indicates that the survivor is not quick to find a new partner. It may, in fact, carry on for year after year in a solitary state. The observations of Goddard in north-eastern New South Wales and my own in Victoria's Ballan-Daylesford Forest concur on this point.

Chapter Six

Big Red Owl of Rain Forest
and Savannah at Australia's Top

A large, striking looking owl, second only in size to the Powerful fellow, and closer to him than it is to the Barking species, will always be beyond the ken of most Australians. This is simply because it dwells in two relatively small strips, apparently isolated from one another, of high rainfall tropical forest, well up Queensland's coast, plus a third and larger band of savannah woodland west of the Gulf of Carpentaria, running from Melville Bay (Northern Territory) across to Admiralty Gulf (Western Australia).

Very little has been recorded of its habits, and in actual fact the Rufous Owl *(Ninox rufa)* could be described as a New Guinea owl, being relatively more numerous over all Papua and New Guinea and Waigeu Island in lowland and lower mountain forest up to 5,500 feet. It dwells also in the Aru Islands. It is the least known of the bigger hawk owls (genus *Ninox*), for our knowledge of it goes little beyond museum skins, and until October 1967 that was the sum total of my own contact with it. In fact the only skin held by the Queensland Museum was collected as far back as 1886 in a gorge of the Herbert River.

The Rufous Owl has not been observed, so far, south of Rockhampton, with the most southerly sight record tabulated at Water Park Creek in that locality (Wolstenholme 1925). This is also the extreme known northern range of the Powerful Owl which was often spoken of by those splendid old-time observers, the Barnards of Coomooboolooroo Station, close by the junction of the Dawson and Mackenzie Rivers, Queensland—some seventy miles inland from Rockhampton. By a stretch of the imagination it would almost seem that the big shots among Australian owls agreed, like warring groups of today, on such a convenient parallel as the Tropic of Capricorn as the 'so far and no further' line.

Though there is an extreme probability of a range overlap between the two big owls thereabouts, the Barnards failed to obtain any evidence of it and indeed very little in the way of rare birds passed their way unnoticed. I well remember Charles Barnard's 1925 contribution to the *Emu* on Birds of Coomooboolooroo, in which he likened the practice of both Winking (Barking) and Powerful Owls in retaining over-night kills such as possums in daylight perches to his well-fed Aboriginal camping companions' habit of gnawing on cooked koala shanks, or some other delicacy like goanna, during wakeful periods at night when already replete.

Sharing the striking characteristic of both Powerful and Barking Owls in having colourful eyes, the Rufous Owl is however not so richly endowed having irides of greenish yellow tint.

The most striking departure from other *Ninox* species, evidently associated with successful specialization for unobtrusive hunting in woodland under tropical conditions, is the inclusive breast and abdominal plumage pattern. Here there is an exceedingly close barring of light brown on an orange-buff background. Ear patches are dark and the tail is well barred.

To me the general, finely-barred ensemble is strongly reminiscent of the overall plumage arrangement in an adult brown Goshawk, and you would never be in any doubt as to identification for no other Australian owl can possibly be confused with the Rufous fellow.

Another of its features shared with Powerful and Barking Owls is a difference in size between male and female, but here the contrast is even more marked. Measurements of museum skins indicate that males are considerably larger than females.

Until 1967 the few notes available referred to a breeding season 'beginning in July', to a habit of perching in dense foliage along watercourses and to hunting at night in adjoining open forest, where a rich variety of small mammals and insects offers an excellent selection among plentiful species of birds.

On 8 September 1916, some fifty years ago, H. G. Barnard discovered a Rufous Owl nest in a dead spout eighty feet high in a tall paper-bark *(Melaleuca)* tree standing in forest near scrub on Meunga Creek, three miles from Cardwell, north Queensland.

Both male and female birds were observed—the hen being smaller and a good deal darker than the male owl. She was flushed from the hollow the day the locality was established (8 September) and on 11 September a climb was undertaken and two eggs at about one week's development were taken. According to Merv Goddard this is the only authentic set of Rufous Owl eggs ever secured and described. From the information it would seem that breeding of these handsome owls begins late in the month of August. In appearance the eggs were of typical round *Ninox* shape, 'midway in size between Powerful and Barking Owl eggs', smooth and glossy white, showing numerous pittings under a lens.

(A)   measured 53 × 44.5 mms.
(B)   measured 54.5 × 44.5 mms.

These measurements were made many years before our discovery of the type set of eggs of the Powerful Owl. Therefore it would appear that Rufous Owl eggs may exceed statistics of those in some clutches of the Powerful Owl. H. G. Barnard probably judged comparative size of Rufous Owl eggs in relation to the false set of '*Ninox strenua*' in the H. L. White collection.

As one would expect from this *Ninox* member, there is reference to a double-syllabled call of low pitch, but whether like Boobook Owls and Barking Owls of the same group it indulges additionally, at times, in some type of screaming note, is something yet to be learned.

Compared with most Australian owls the Rufous fellow has a somewhat limited range and is evidently a 'stayput' within the confines of chosen habitats. Therefore under such circumstances it is not so strange that three definite races of the bird are recognized in the three distinct areas of known habitation isolated from one another by geographical and botanical features in the north.

West of the Carpentaria Gulf along the extreme top of Australia from Admiralty Gulf, Western Australia to Melville Bay, Northern Territory, dwells *Ninox rufa rufa* which from wing measurements of eleven specimens supplied by Mees (1964) is definitely the largest member of the clan. Interestingly, measurement for measurement, the size shows a comparatively close approach to that of the Powerful Owl.

The next area of distribution along the eastern side of Cape York in Queensland, running as far south as Cardwell, holds *Ninox rufa marginata* which is conspicuously smaller. Its type specimen collected in 1916 by H. G. Barnard at Cardwell, is in the H. L. White skin collection housed by the National Museum of Victoria. In this case, Mees' wing measurements of males are only a few millimetres in excess of those of average New South Wales and south Queensland male Barking Owls. Finally 200 miles further south, apparently separated by a drier zone from the north-eastern rain forests of *Ninox rufa marginata,* is the third Rufous Owl habitat of Mackay-Fitzroy River area which future observations may extend to points even further south. Similar in size to *N. rufa marginata,* this *N. rufa queenslandica* was established as such by Mathews as far back as 1911. Mees (1964) admits the danger of creating a subspecies on the basis of a single museum skin, but emphasizes that the Mackay female bird examined (in the possession of New York's American Museum of Natural History) is so much darker on back, head and wings with colder brown cross-bands on the under surface and darker cheeks altogether that there is no option but to admit it as a separate race. He adds that the Water Park Creek sighting published by Wolstenholme in 1925 must also belong to this particular race of Rufous Owl. Before leaving the interesting variations of this tropical species, it should be noted also that the New Guinea and Aru Islands birds are defined as two more separate races.

In campfire yarns while observing Barking Owls in the Gin Gin area, I had often discussed the Rufous Owl with Eric Zillmann. Ways and means of finding this bird, for which the Queensland Primary Industries Department Fauna Officer (Mr C. Roff) had kindly arranged a limited collecting permit, were always to the fore; but because of year-round commitments (animals in my case) I was never able to take either the low road or the high road, so that Eric reached north Queensland before me.

He did very well indeed, getting on to a locality where Mr Lindsay Bates, Schoolmaster of Mareeba, had originally pinpointed two Rufous Owls and later shown them to Bruce Cook, also of that town. In turn, in September 1965 Bruce Cook took Mr Zillmann to this mountainous spot less than twenty miles from Mareeba, where the timber, with the exception of stream valleys, was neither tall nor dense (some forty to fifty feet average). Unfortunately there was no one 'at home' in the perching gully and it took a further visit by Eric Zillmann later that month to disclose the whereabouts of a lone single bird. However, there it sat—a fair dinkum, yellow-eyed Rufous Owl—'one of the most striking birds of prey I've ever seen' to quote from the enthusiastic letter subsequently written by Mr Zillmann.

The exciting owl was perched immediately over the running water of a stream in the gully and therefore no traces of pellets and little of the whitewash indicative of habitual residence could be found.

Returning that way in May 1966, Mr Zillmann had the further thrill of locating the pair perched in the same spot some two feet apart. Most unfortunately, by the time his camera was ready, one owl had flown off but he observed and photographed the other from a distance of only thirty feet.

Significantly Mr Zillmann's comment that both birds appeared similar in size would seem to indicate that the larger size of males, so very evident in measurement of museum skins, may be variable and certainly is not always apparent in living specimens of the middle group *(N. rufa marginata)*.

Understandably in attempting this book on Australian owls I was somewhat up in the air over the *rufous* species of which, personally, as mentioned, I had had no experience whatever.

Official permission from the Primary Industries Department made it legal to secure a living pair, but as the only known nesting performance by these birds was that recorded by H. G. Barnard fifty years ago on Meunga Creek, Cardwell, there was a vast gulf between Government sanction and accomplished fact.

However, in late October 1967, after I had written the foregoing notes, Eric Zillmann scored a dramatic success which changed the whole situation. By excellent bushmanship and keen observation he located Rufous Owls nesting in the neighbourhood of a granitic timbered creek of intermittent clear pools—not so far from Mount Mulligan, North Queensland. Plentiful whitewash, scattered glider fur and pellets within a limited area led the searcher to investigate intensively along a belt of trees on both sides of the permanent watercourse. On the second day of zig-zagging he caught sight of a whitish owlet perched at the rim of a hollow, 65 feet up in a not-so-big (six-foot-diameter trunk) forest red gum.

That, of course, really fired the starting gun, and Paul Gallagher drove, flew and ran to the scene, all 1,300 miles from Burleigh, bearing as luggage only the indispensable rope ladder. Meantime, while awaiting reinforcements, Mr Zillmann witnessed an amazing drama of savage attack in broad daylight by the owls upon a trespassing goanna. The would-be marauder and scavenger of tell-tale skeletal material dropped by the owls was practically lifted off the tree and put to ignominious flight.

Fledgling Rufous Owl first seen by Eric Zillmann perched at the entrance spout of a hollow 65 feet above ground. Partly blind, the owlet fell almost to earth. Antics of bristling, beak-snapping and wing-raising are similar in all members of the genus Ninox.

A distinguished bird baby. Rufous Owlet at nest-leaving stage, showing opaque left eye and spotted iris of right eye. Because of near-blindness (since remedied) the bird would certainly have perished had it not been picked up and treated with antibiotics.

Rufous Owl in daytime perch immediately over running stream in a gully 20 miles from Mareeba, north Queensland. The general finely-barred breast ensemble is clearly seen. Photo Eric Zillmann.

There was anticlimax before the ascent of the tree with the tumble to within eighteen feet of the ground of the owlet. The misguided venturesomeness of this sole occupant of the nursery evidently tied in with sight defects, involving a semi-opaque iris of the left eye with similar though less evident spotting in the other. Both eyes have since responded one hundred per cent to antibiotic treatment and vitamin A addition to diet.

These Rufous parents shamed all other Australian owls with the exception of the Barking species, by launching unhesitating reprisals on the climbers investigating the nest. Messrs Zillmann and Gallagher were united in voicing their uneasiness under constant threat of talon strikes while swaying about in mid-air. Certainly the scratches inflicted through Paul's shirt bore witness to whole-hearted attack. We have no record whatever of any such retaliation under similar circumstances by the Powerful Owl, though similarly the murmur, rumble, or grating expression of anxiety used with variations by all *Ninox* members accompanied the Rufous Owl actions.

The nesting hole itself was very small, penetrating three feet into the tree's interior through a triangular entrance. It contained little in the way of pellets, but strips of skin and fur, both here and on top of a favoured feeding termitarium 'platform' close to ground level, could have been those of squirrel-gliders captured during nocturnal forays in neighbouring open eucalypt forest. This consisted of trees averaging fifty feet or so in height.

The close relationship of Rufous to Powerful Owls was graphically illustrated by a recording on tape made by Mr Zillmann of *Ninox rufa*'s voice, though here again the fact that this proceeding could be accomplished *within sight* of the subject points to a much more assertive and equable temperament.

The 'woo-hoo!' 'oo-hoo!' or 'woo-woo!'—possibly that of the deeper-voiced (?) male Rufous—is somewhat softer and not so far carrying as that of a Powerful Owl, and the bird concerned lapsed after a time into similarly spaced single notes. Otherwise the voice was practically identical with that of a male Powerful Owl—so much so that it would probably bring about retaliatory measures in Powerful Owl territory.* It would also be extremely difficult to distinguish between the calls in borderline country, unless the

---

* This theory is now an established fact. Nocturnal playing of the taped Rufous Owl voice at McLeod's Creek (November 1967) brought about the prompt arrival of an irate Powerful Owl female and a well grown owlet.

occasional single note calling is a consistent feature of Rufous Owl vocabulary. There is nothing of the quick-firing explosive quality characteristic of the Barking Owl.

Healthy on arrival in spite of its temporary visual handicap, the beak-snapping owlet weighed a mere twenty ounces, and with the exception of pale rufous finely-barred back and wing feathering it was clothed in dazzling snow-white down which left even Powerful owlets of similar age dark by comparison.

Now, 4 November 1967, the clear eyes are pale yellowish-green with an overall triangular mascara'd appearance due to dark adjoining ear patches, while the downy forehead has developed a ginger patch and the toes are lemon yellow. However the shrill trilling call is more that of a young Barking Owl than the thin high-pitched voice of a fledgling Powerful Owl. Continued observations on the rare youngster promise much of interest, and meantime it has teamed with a similarly aged Barking owlet—both birds perching together by daylight regularly and displaying a good deal of similarity, not only in 'words' but in flight antics and the fascinating play of head winding and survey from every conceivable angle.

A true pair of Rufous Owls, in which the male bird is decidedly darker than the female, is now (August 1971) happily housed for nesting purposes at West Burleigh Reserve.

They were secured, under permit in the Mareeba district, Q. by Eric Zillmann on October 25 1970—the older bird being then no more than 17 days old.

Thanks to an upbringing from such a tender age these birds are as domesticated as one could possibly wish.

Chapter Seven

The Vociferous Barking Owl
and the Truth about Screams
in the Night

Without doubt the sturdy Barking Owl, smaller cousin of the Powerful and Rufous Owls, is near enough to the big fellows to qualify as a species of the same genus *(Ninox connivens)*, yet psychologically it is as different from the Powerful Owl as proverbial chalk is from cheese—an extrovert of the open places as compared with an introvert of the hidden mountain gullies.

This chunky, robust, greyish-brown owl, some 27 oz. in weight, for which I have a tremendous affection and enthusiasm, might well be described as the outstanding personality among Australian night birds.

Certainly it is the most vociferous, irrepressible and cheerful of our owls and one of the mighty hunters of the time. Known as the Winking Owl in the official checklist and in various bird books, this strong, golden-eyed bird actually does not blink or wink any more than do other Australian owls. Perhaps the first one encountered was merely reacting to a foreign body in an eye. It is, however, a particularly noisy exponent of a gruff, almost explosive, double 'bark'; so much like that of a dog in the case of the male that one can be excused for drawing incorrect conclusions. I suggest, therefore, and I am sure all familiar with the bird will agree, that 'Barking Owl', as a truly appropriate name, should be adopted. I have always advocated that name, and find it enjoys priority over 'Winking Owl', having been used more than a century ago—see *Emu*, Vol. 41, January 1942, p. 233.

Widely spread over Australia, with the exception of a big section of the centre and west, this versatile owl is sparse in its distribution and certainly a most handsome member of the genus *Ninox*. For its size—at least twice that of the rich brown Boobook Owl *(N. novaeseelandiae boobook)*—it is one of the most efficient winged predators.

In his excellent revision of Australian owls from a critical examination of skins in museum collections both in and out of the country, Dr G. F. Mees *Zool. Verh.* no. 65 (1964) described three races of Australian Barking Owls—one on Cape York, another belonging to the Northern Territory and the third, which is the largest and darkest race *(N. connivens connivens,* featured here) inhabiting the eastern side of Australia, most of Queensland and a small portion of south-western Australia. Strangely, no Barking Owl exists in Tasmania, Kangaroo Island or Melville Island.

Reared from infancy Barking Owls exhibit remarkable affection and intelligence. They are naturally semi-diurnal and I have watched them dive on incautious birds in strong sunlight. In fact, on a hot glaring afternoon not so long ago, visitors watching one of our Queensland Barking Owls weaving its head from side to side as the golden eyes concentrated upon a point of interest below, were amazed when the stocky bird launched itself in a lightning dive. There was a strangled squeak as it seized a furry object in a grassy corner, and in no time the owl was back on its perch clutching a black rat that had paid the price of an imprudent visit.

Naturally the onlookers voiced incredulity at the ready perception in sunlight and swift follow-up by the nocturnal hunter, for, to this day, the popular and erroneous belief that owls are blind in daytime dies hard. Surprisingly enough, on a really black night the soft-winged birds can be almost as helpless in the dark as we are and at such times they perch, hour by hour, in one spot waiting for moonrise or the dawn light to show them the way to go home.

Naturally under poor lighting conditions owls' eyes do have an undoubted sensitivity, and as complete blackness at night is the exception rather than the rule, the birds hunt quite easily in the dim light of the stars or moon, or at dusk and dawn.

This extra sensitivity is achieved with the loss of certain refinements found in day birds, such as colour vision and fine resolution of detail (cone cells). Nevertheless an owl's eye is packed tight with rod cells which contain a remarkable chemical called visual purple which converts even a glimmer of light into a chemical signal, giving the bird an actual sight impression where the human eye would detect only the presence of light. There is an increase in the brightness of the image formed by the lens and, as we well know, the large size and fixed nature of the forwardly-directed eyes are the most striking feature of an owl's anatomy. They necessitate the characteristic 'revolving' head movement, which is such an attractive and fascinating habit. Few species stand higher than eighteen inches, yet the eyes of many are bigger than our own.

Brilliant sunshine irritates most of them and causes the same pin-pointing of eye pupils as occurs in cats or in your camera when avoiding an over-exposure.

Certainly, however, Barking Owls are far more versatile in daylight than most of their kindred and, in my opinion, could be trained as falcons, excellent for use at any time around the clock.

It is a fairly common occurrence for these solidly built birds to kill and eat ring-tailed possums, sugar-gliders and squirrel-gliders. They prey upon small birds, medium birds, magpies, rabbits, young hares, rats and mice.

Something of the incredible variety of diet characteristic of the American Horned Owl *(Bubo virginianus)* creeps in here, for a pellet brought from a Barking Owl hollow on the Clarence River by Merv Goddard (1965) and investigated by Queensland Museum staff, consisted not only of remains of at least two sugar-gliders, unidentified post-cranial matter and insect remains, but also of fish spines.

One Barking Owl brought to me with a broken wing following the spiking of its shoulder on a barbed-wire fence, killed and ate a healthy Frogmouth in the space of a single night. Later experiences in Queensland indicate that the poor Frogmouths are favourite victims, indeed, and below perches in sheokes on St Agnes Creek near Gin Gin, where these nocturnal bushrangers habitually rest, there are generally Frogmouth feathers, while the fur or feather-wrapped pellets, normally disgorged six to ten hours following a meal, contain squirrel-glider remains, beetle wing cases, rat material and bones of Magpie Larks, Choughs and other birds. Held in the spotlight beam during our night visits to them, the St Agnes birds glared unblinkingly in haughty indignation, snapping their beaks while the golden eyes reflected the light.

One evening in November 1941, Mr McInnes of Nanneela, via Rochester, Victoria, watched a flock of Wild Duck pitch on a water hole. No sooner did they alight than a Barking Owl swooped down, seized one in its talons, and flew with it to the rail of a fence. The owls—particularly the males—lift 'heavy' burdens with surprising ease. Their toes and talons are disproportionately large, and I guarantee that anyone incautiously handling one of them and experiencing that agonizing retaliatory clutch by merciless talons will remember the accident for ever more. To be caught in like manner by a Powerful Owl is, of course, far more serious and a truly frightful predicament, which many years ago resulted in the Powerful Owl originally earning its title, when an early collector wounded a specimen and made an incautious approach.

Although the Barking Owl may dwell and rest in, or immediately adjoining, the larger scrubs and heavy forests—I observed a pair feeding owlets on the Gibbo River between Benambra and Corryong, Victoria, and you will find them camping in Queensland coastal rain forests adjoining 'outside' hunting areas—the bird, in inland Victoria and New South Wales, is typically an inhabitant of the more open savannah woodland, particularly along water-course timber and scattered clumps of box trees. Northern Victoria's Murray Valley areas and the Hume Highway country from Seymour to Wodonga represent the characteristic country of *Ninox connivens*.

In the mid–1930s my interest in and speculation about the blood-curdling screams, allegedly uttered at times by the Powerful Owl, was at an extremely high pitch. In spite of quite lengthy experience with the larger owl we had no shred of evidence to tie the screaming notes to it. Also in those days in Victoria, as a writer of Nature Notes in the Melbourne *Argus* and *Australasian,* I had received a number of 'screaming woman' reports from the Wimmera, Murray River districts and other northern Victorian areas.

None of these cries could have emanated from Powerful Owls, for such open localities were totally at variance with the dark secluded gullies and dense timber environment of *Ninox strenua.* However, such places *are* typical haunts of the Barking Owl which, with its yellow eyes, yellow toes and general appearance, suggests a Powerful Owl on a smaller scale. It was with a suspicion that this so-called Winking Owl had something to do with the frightening nocturnal screeches, that I looked forward to listening to birds of the species over a lengthy period in captivity.

For a number of years, a pair of them had made their headquarters in the scattered timber about 'Glenroy' homestead on the comparatively bare plains of Womboota, New South Wales. In the late spring of 1937 Mr J. R. Goodisson, owner of 'Glenroy', dis-covered the nesting site of the owls *at ground level* inside the leaning trunk of an old grey box tree. The entrance to the deep hollow was seven feet above the ground. Thanks to the observations and help of Mr Goodisson, three well-grown owlets were taken from this tree in December 1937, and established in an aviary at the Heales-ville Sanctuary. In their care the motto was 'nothing but the best' and the time and effort lavished on these distinguished, wondering-eyed guests were considerable.

During early winter nights of the following year the character-istic call notes of the species gradually became quite a feature of the fauna reserve. The rapid double bark uttered with closed beak resembles 'woop-woop', 'wook-wook' or 'wuk-wuk', according to the fancy of the listener, and *there is a considerable difference between the pitch of male and female voices.* In fact, the calls of cock and hen bird form an alternating 'quick firing' accompaniment and are given with more vigour than those of any other night bird I have ever heard. The gruff, low-pitched, remarkably dog-like 'wook-wook' of the male bird is followed quickly by the higher 'wok-wok' of the hen, and so they continue until there is a sudden ces-sation. Though not heard at a distance, it is noticeable at close quarters that these abrupt calls work up from peculiar growling notes resembling 'er-wook-wook' until, following several repeti-tions, the fore-running growl is dropped and the clear double call runs loudly in top gear. Conversely, the double call may drop back into the growling stage. In my experience no other Australian owl has such a clearly defined vocal differentiation between the sexes.

Male Barking Owls are baritones and females sopranos, resulting during normal conversation in extreme clarity over a greater distance in the case of the female owl.

It is no exaggeration to claim that the deep, gruff, double bark of the male bird penetrates over a mere half of the area in which the female may be heard. In fact at times it is so difficult to pick up the male bird's voice that one is left with the impression that only the hen owl is calling.

The birds, which normally dwell in pairs in their haunts, usually begin their barking calls early in the evening, often before it is dark. At times during the night barking calls are again heard, but most curious habit of all, which I have noted quite often while camped in the vicinity of Barking Owl home sites, is the farewell early morning chorus, uttered in broad daylight before the birds retire to perch in foliage. The owls do not appear to seek any great protection in daytime and may be heard 'barking' at any time of the day. In fact, the Barking Owl is more noisy and more at home in daytime than any other Australian night bird I have met.

There appears to be the odd bird that has either lost its mate or turns upon its kind, resulting in territorial calling which is fantastic in its unflagging monotony.

A notable example roosted for a couple of years in semi-rain forest in the Noosa River vicinity neighbouring Kin Kin, Queensland. She was a Barking Owl we referred to during taipan hunts as 'the hysterical female' and though investigated night and day over several nesting seasons (and we had to cut tracks to her with machetes), she was never seen with a mate and to our knowledge never laid eggs. However, she 'wok-wok'd' incessantly just as did an apparently elderly pair at Hugh Innes' Walla Station on the Burnett River. We never knew this pair to nest, either, but at any nocturnal mimicry of their cries they would arrive promptly to defend the territory. Possibly Mr Innes sent them 'round the bend' because of his constant mimicry and their consequent ricochetting back and forth like yo-yos from a rain forest island across the river to and from the Walla homestead.

My friend Hugh even took to greeting his friends and knocking at doors calling 'wook-wook'. Nearly all of us went round the bend to some extent, odd ones like me to stay for keeps!

Remarkable to relate, the lone Noosa River female neighboured a permanent pair of her kind a mile to the north, with another pair dwelling only half a mile to the south-west—both in patches of rain forest.

Usually Barking Owls attain their second season before they set up house and lay the usual clutch of three eggs (end of July to mid-August) but a pair named 'Hughie' and 'Little Mattie', located as babies by that keen observer Eric Zillmann on Gin Gin Creek, made history by not only producing eggs at the startling age of ten and a half months but successfully rearing owlets.

As in the case of the Powerful Owl the male is a bigger and more powerful bird than the female, reversing the rule so general in birds of prey and particularly in the Masked Owls of Australia.

One dark night in March 1939, during a prowl along Healesville

Opposite: *Five to six weeks old Barking Owlets. They are unique in possessing mottled breast down much after the pattern of the future feather plumage.*

'Associated with the hen owl's retirement, the cock Barking Owl became extra-ordinarily savage. It was positively dangerous to enter without the protection of a long-handled broom.' So dog-like is the male Barking Owl's double bark that more than once the author has awakened in the small hours under an impression of a canine raid on the Fauna Reserve.

Aggressiveness of the cock Barking Owl at nesting time has to be seen to be believed. Once he drove his talons deep into the back of my hand. I then took to wearing a thick overcoat capped by a milk bucket 'helmet'—even so, the crash was stunning!

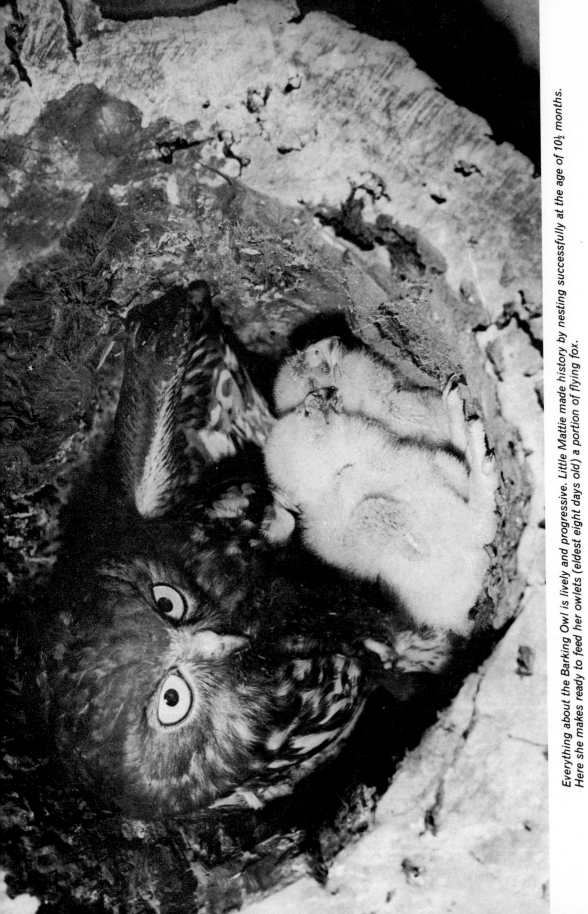

Everything about the Barking Owl is lively and progressive. Little Mattie made history by nesting successfully at the age of 10½ months. Here she makes ready to feed her owlets (eldest eight days old) a portion of flying fox.

Sanctuary tracks in armed search of marauding cats and foxes, I heard a loud, startling, tremulous scream repeated three or four times, at intervals of perhaps ten seconds. It came from away down in the Barking Owl aviary vicinity and suggested a woman's voice calling 'h–e–l–p'; it was both weird, urgent and hair raising.

At long last strong conviction grew that the Barking Owl was indeed the 'screaming woman' of the long years of mystery. That was indeed a memorable and exciting evening. However, following this one performance the birds clammed up. It was not until the 1940 season after the owls had been two and a half years with us that I became absolutely sure, from the indisputable evidence of several close range nocturnal performances, that this species is truly the 'screeching woman' of northern Victorian areas and elsewhere where the cries have been so often reported.

The fact that these screams are only heard occasionally, and mainly during the months of March and April (late autumn), is interesting in bearing out the mysterious nature and rare use of this particular call note. Uttered with open beak, it is exactly what one imagines a girl or woman would utter on perceiving some object inspiring abject terror. It is single, loud and forcefully given, and may be repeated eight or nine times at intervals of about ten seconds, or, on some occasions, with minutes between each performance. There is no chorus of screams but simply the rising tremulous, high note.

The rarity of the Barking Owl's wavering scream is borne out by Mr Goodisson's experiences before the Badger Creek owls were obtained. During a number of years' residence at Womboota, he heard the birds 'barking' regularly, but his recollections of the drawn-out screaming cries were few indeed, and he had heard this performance mostly at a distance.

Dwelling now in Queensland, thirty years after collecting those fascinating first Barking Owls at Womboota, and with the additional experience of both this species and the Powerful Owl in the field in northern New South Wales and south-eastern Queensland, I think I can be quite dogmatic in claiming that the Barking Owl screams, whereas the Powerful Owl does not.

In case it may be thought that either the Barn Owl, the Masked Owl in its various forms, or the Sooty Owl could be responsible, we have had each and all of them under close observation for year after year. The results are entirely negative as far as this special scream is concerned.

Meticulous Mervyn Goddard of Tenterfield, long time authority on birds of prey, and probably the greatest tree-climber Australia has ever produced, knows more Powerful Owl nesting sites than any other living man and he supports these conclusions without reservation.

However, a final point must be made clear and that is the undoubted fact that *it is the hen Barking Owl with her soprano voice who really shines in performance of the banshee scream.* The seven or eight tremulous high-pitched wails of 'h-e-l-p!', eerily human, are uttered with open beak and achieve maximum demoralizing effect should the bird be passing over at night on the wing. She, and not he, is the culprit it took so many eventful years finally to run to earth.

Why, it may be asked, do they scream? Certainly it is a feature of the fall of the year and the exciting courting time when the birds may be temporarily afield from one another, for it is a cry that carries further than the 'wook-wook' notes. With variations it is employed to intimidate trespassers at the nesting site and is a well calculated deterrent to creatures possibly menacing new-fledged young. Finally, believe it or not, it occasionally expresses fright caused by the arrival of a predatory animal such as a dingo, fox or goanna.

Eighteen months after the arrival of the birds from Womboota, a fourth adult specimen which had been injured by a car near Beaufort, Victoria, was rescued and forwarded to me at Healesville by Lady White, of Middle Creek. This hen owl soon recovered, and, though rather nervous, she gradually settled down to new conditions and the plentiful diet of rats and rabbits upon which all were fed.

Both in 1939 and 1940, clutches of eggs had been laid by a Womboota bird in a hollow log in the aviary, but without successful results. Early in 1941 a special enclosure was constructed in peppermint bush completely out of the way of public pathways and disturbances of any kind, and there a male Barking Owl and the Middle Creek hen bird were established on their own. Subsequent results in both the new aviary and the original one, each of which now housed a pair of the birds, were sufficient justification for the move. The aviary in the patch of peppermint timber was not far from my home, consequently it was not difficult to keep the birds under close observation both by day and night.

During early winter their barking calls were heard nightly, but during the first weeks of July they practically ceased loud calling altogether. At close quarters, single hoarse notes and rumbling peevish notes from the hen were occasionally heard; it was evident from this and the actions of the larger cock bird in spending a good deal of time, both night and day, in scraping a depression in the rotten wood of a large hollow log suspended from the roof, that nesting operations had commenced. On 24 July the hen bird laid her first egg in the spot prepared by the cock bird. A complete clutch of three appeared, with an interval of nearly three days between the laying of each egg. The female owl sat closely from the day prior to the appearance of her first egg. which explains the considerable difference in age and size noticed later in her family. Her only emergences were for a few minutes soon after dusk, when she uttered her peevish rumbling calls for food and put on the most miserable appearance possible.

Associated with the hen's retirement, the cock owl became extraordinarily savage. It was positively dangerous to enter the aviary without the protection of a long-handled broom. On one occasion the bird drove his long, keen talons through the large mesh netting and scored my arm while I was looking in from the outside. Another day he drove his claws deep into the back of my hand. Septic results followed two days later, necessitating additional anti-tetanus injections. The pugnacity of the male bird, with his fierce attacks, accompanied by loud snapping of his bill, and the absolute refusal of the female bird to be scared off her nest, are typical characteristics of the species in general. Wild Barking Owls act very similarly and after dark at one nesting site my hat was violently swiped from my head.

Nesting sites vary considerably: from Roy Goodisson's ground level site at Womboota in the sparsest of savannah timber, up to a height of ninety-five feet recorded by Merv Goddard in 1966 in heavy blackbutt forest near Grafton, New South Wales.

On 30 August the first Healesville owlet was hatched and the third came out six days later. Thus the incubation period for each was approximately thirty-seven days. Each time a ladder commanding a view of the hollow log 'nursery' was climbed, both male and female birds screamed in the curious fashion so seldom heard on normal occasions. The hen owl shrieked and snapped her bill from her brooding position, closely covering her offspring, which she could not be induced to leave. Their shrill voices trilled away beneath her feathers. On 9 September when the eldest was eleven days old, the 'borrowing' of the owlets for the purposes of a photograph was a most hazardous operation, and I had to call in an assistant to ward off savage aerial attack.

In fact, to avoid personal damage and serious facial injuries in particular, I took to wearing a thick overcoat capped by a solid milk bucket 'helmet'. Even so, the crash of the solid $1\frac{3}{4}$ lb. male owl against my metal headpiece was stunning enough in all conscience.

The little fellows at this stage showed few indications of their later charming appearance, but a picture obtained at the time shows clearly the disparity in size due to the difference in times of hatching.

From the age of a fortnight onwards the owlets developed rapidly and strongly in spite of the insanitary state of the hollow log nest. Pieces of rabbit, rats and, in one instance, a ring-tailed possum that had foolishly squeezed through the wire netting at night were not wholly eaten. Usually the 'appetizing' portions were plucked off and supplied, whilst odd remains lay about the hollow and under the youngsters. However, such a state of affairs is more or less typical of owls in general, though conditions here are never as bad as with members of the Masked group.

At the age of nineteen days it was evident that the white fluff of the older owlets was giving place to a general greyish-coloured down and the irides of the eyes, previously greenish in tinge, were showing first signs of the coming golden yellow. On that day (17 September) I removed the owlets from their parents—experiencing the expected savage attack in doing so. From that stage onwards I reared them at home by hand, with the result that three months later the young owls became the most delightful, confiding, intelligent and interesting feathered creatures it has ever been my pleasure to observe.

This is no idle claim for I have reared youngsters of most species of Australian eagles, hawks and owls.

However, step by step with this family, the other Barking Owls in the original aviary advanced also. The eggs of this pair of birds were laid on the same dates and the first owlet hatched on the same day as that on which the first 'triplet' broke its way from the shell in the newer aviary. In this case, however, only the first and evidently the strongest owlet survived. This little family was not interfered with, and from it the date on which the mother finally left the owlet to its own devices and resumed normal roosting habits was learned. This occurred on 27 September, when the owlet was twenty-nine days of age.

By this time all four owlets were clothed in light-greyish down with grey and white striations on chest and abdomen, closely resembling the adult feather pattern. A nearly complete whitish collar also distinguishes them from this time on until they lose it at the age of two and a half months.

Some truly precocious owlets of the species have been heard to utter falsetto squeaking 'wook-wooks' at this very age, but though these fellows may have so 'spoken' to their parents, they were more dignified with me using only the urgent, somewhat grating trill which is deeper and less cricket-like than the voices of baby Boobook Owls.

The talons of the Barking Owlets were by now noticeably sharp and the effect upon any hand the soft-plumaged birds chose for a perch was painful indeed.

The 'triplets' at home were becoming increasingly active and playful. Their rolling voices were continuous, and, with heads winding about even upside down on 'rubber' necks, their antics were comical indeed.

The owlet still with its parents was first observed right out of the hollow on 3 October, the day it was exactly five weeks old. The young birds, with the exception of the undersized baby, could now flutter a few feet and daily, from that time on, their wings gained power. At six weeks of age the larger ones flew quite well, but the smaller bird was not strong on the wing until late in October when it was at least seven weeks old. Indications, later proved to be fact, pointed to it as the only female bird of the four owlets.

The appetites of the young birds were enormous. I was kept unusually busy hunting game and it was not at all uncommon for my three 'foster children' to devour a half-grown rabbit overnight between them—fur, bones, stomach and intestines—and then demand more food in the morning. In this greedy gulping down of the entire viscera of prey, the young birds differed markedly from adults, which discard stomach and intestines most carefully.

Late in November, when the youngsters were approaching the age of three months, the slate grey feathering and mottled grey and white of the under-surface began to supersede the immature downy plumage of the owlets. At four months the change-over was complete, even to the sturdy grey-feathered legs in the older owlets, though the smallest bird was still lagging behind in development.

Except for their whistling voices, which would not 'break' for another month or so, the bigger birds were by then indistinguishable in appearance from an adult. They were indeed fascinating, lively creatures, ready to perch on my head, shoulders or arms, whistling continuously, whenever I entered the enclosure. To frighten them was nearly impossible.

I liberated the pair that raised the single owlet and these two, accompanied by the youngster, told the world about their new experiences in dog-like barking that echoed throughout the bush both night and day.

On the second night, however, there was a terrific disturbance among roosting magpies and I rather suspected the owls were not confining their attentions to the rabbits. Fortunately they soon moved on to a more acceptable habitat.

It was a far cry from these Riverina Barking Owls to their colleagues in the Gin Gin district of Queensland, but it became a habit of the 1950s to camp periodically along St Agnes Creek on Hugh Innes' 'Walla' station, right below the water gum *(Eugenia* sp.) stronghold of a well-known pair. It was always enthralling to take in their cheerful conversation at night and the goodbyes in the dawn light as they overlapped the sweet songs of Jackie Winters heralding a new day. How many things in life are so truly free.

Renewal of acquaintance with these Barking Owls in the water gums and sheokes of the chronically dry stream bed, after an absence, often began a conversation of lively diurnal 'wook-wooks'. We felt almost related to these personality birds, considering their children and grandchildren had been in our care for so many Barking Owl generations.

Some seasons (August-September-October) there were no nesting signs at all, and maybe odd lean goannas that Dot, my little dog, chased up near-by gums could have supplied the answer.

In their armour-plated suits even Barking Owl talons could scarcely deter bandits of such tree-scaling ability and, of course, appearances by the owls themselves aimed at repelling boarders in daylight quickly attract additional hazards such as harrying antics by raucous crows.

Of the many Barking Owls from Gin Gin and elsewhere we have kept and bred over the years (actually since 1937 we have had them continuously, with three pairs at present), at least twenty-five offspring have been liberated and among the youngsters there have been some outstanding personalities.

'Elizabeth'—namesake of the youngest daughter of Mr and Mrs Hugh Innes at 'Walla'—was perhaps the most conversational owl of all time.

Hand-reared from the eight-day stage and completely anthropocentric, she would 'wok-wok!' impartially to all and sundry, day or night. To her, all members of *Homo sapiens* were Barking Owls, so with little or no encouragement she talked freely to anything wearing clothes. Her fame at our Burleigh Fauna Reserve was such that people who knew of her, by hearsay, paid special visits for exclusive 'interviews'. Not only did she converse with them but flew close to the wire netting for thorough get-together chats. So completely did this amazing bird adapt herself to human companionship that when unrelated young Barkers, housed near by, lost their trilling baby voices and began to utter the adult 'wook-wook'—the female in the same key as herself—she felt her territory domination had been challenged and, thoroughly infuriated, began to call the whole night long. Naturally, with this lusty and monotonous barking running non-stop, it became necessary to move the younger female to temporary quarters beyond Elizabeth's sphere of 'influence'. This happened to be an aviary beneath our Queensland house but unfortunately the banished owl also developed an attack of the 'wok-woks', and on her first and last night of nocturnal sing-song there, no one slept particularly well.

Most famous of these domesticated Barking Owls was 'Andy', a humourist and vocalist of high degree, upon whom I spent rewarding time in the days of his infancy. His gruff, explosive double call was part of our lives, first of all at Healesville in Victoria, and later at Burleigh Heads, Queensland, for he was a grandson of the original Womboota birds.

I shall never forget the evening I had promised to give a lecture on owls to the Bird Observers' Club of Victoria in Flinders Street Railway Building, Melbourne. Andy accompanied me in the back of the panel van, travelling at ease inside his special first class case. The spectacle of this blasé fellow sitting on a rostrum vigorously winding his head at the audience in inimitable owl fashion, charming it with his great expressive golden eyes and finally electrifying them with a succession of quick-firing 'wook-wooks', was truly something out of this world.

On this particular evening of heavy traffic and failing light, I was stopped by red traffic signals in the heart of the city at a busy intersection. Sitting at the wheel with engine idling I heard Andy mutter 'wook-wook', and absent-mindedly, as a matter of course, called 'wook-wook' loudly a number of times in reply. As Andy took the matter still further I happened to catch the glance of a parallel driver, also awaiting the green light. Obviously he had already persuaded himself I was an escapee from the nut house. When you consider the matter his odd expression was quite excusable. After all, normal drivers do not usually gaze into space calling 'wook-wook' in loud determined tones in heavy city traffic.

Temporarily quartered below the tall house at West Burleigh in the autumn of 1952, and doubtless stimulated by entirely new surroundings, Andy gave vent to the occasional anguished shrieks for which his kind now gets its due.

It was his unexpected and repeated full-dress rehearsal of a strangled scream that panicked an unknown, inebriated gentleman who called upon us at a midnight hour enquiring the way to go home. He descended those steps backwards, after which we never saw him again.

Andy could be stimulated by the sudden ringing of a Condamine cowbell to turn on a scream even in daytime, but unfortunately we never recorded a performance and, of course, for full effect, the cry of a hen Barking Owl in flight is the real McCoy.

Sometimes Andy went bush, but never for keeps, and he took to perching on a rail high up on the front verandah. In early morning light he would return to camp a mere jump ahead of an indignant horde of assorted Butcher Birds, Magpies, Noisy Miners (Mickies) and Smaller Honey-eaters, to rumble derisively at them when he got there.

On a steamy black night of pouring rain in February 1956, a marauding carpet python from the surrounding bush brought an end to this association of such long and happy standing. The constrictor found a way into Andy's aviary and wrapped about him. Sad to say, it was too late when we got there and Andy's mortal remains now repose in the Queensland Museum. The evenings were sadly quiet for a long, long time afterwards. As long as I live I shall never forget him.

Eldest owlet at eight days old. Both these Barking Owl babies still have prominent egg breakers on their beaks. Their toes are chubby with small talons feebly developed.

Barking Owlets. 'On 9 September 1941 when the eldest was eleven days old, "borrowing" of the owlets for the purposes of a photograph was a most hazardous operation.'

J. R. Goodisson, former owner of 'Glenroy Estate', Womboota, N.S.W., with the
triplet Barking Owlets taken from the grey box hollow (Dec. 1937). Much was
learned from them.

Opposite: Grey box (Eucalyptus hemiphloia) nesting site of Barking Owls, on the
bare plains of Womboota, N.S.W. The entrance hole is located at the spot where
J. R. Goodisson holds the owlets, with nest chamber at ground level inside.

Barking Owl triplets close to nest-leaving stage (five weeks) show a nearly complete whitish collar, which they lose at the age of 2½ months.

First Barking Owlet family hatched in captivity (1941). There is a difference of six days between the youngest and eldest. 'They became the most delightful, confiding, intelligent and interesting feathered creatures it has ever been my pleasure to observe.'

Twin Barking Owlets five weeks old. Incomplete whitish collars of nest-leaving stage and the unique mottling of breast down are obvious.

J. R. Goodisson, former owner of 'Glenroy Estate', Womboota, N.S.W., with the triplet Barking Owlets (taken December 1937) from which so much was learned.

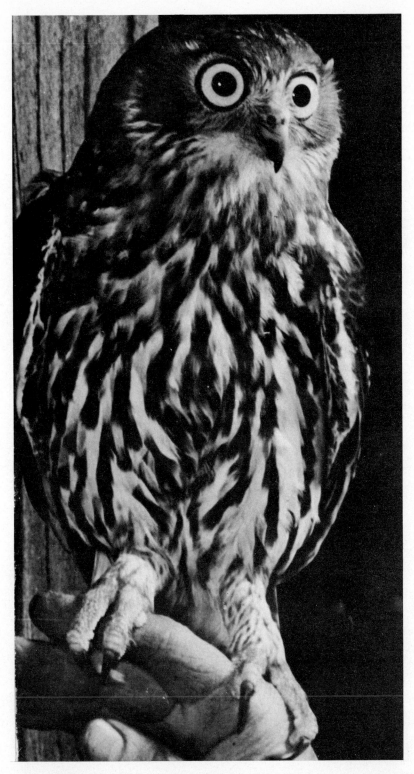

Andy, the Barking Owl—a humorist and vocalist of high degree, who performed magnificently with barking notes and head winding antics when used as a living example of his kind in lecture halls.

Alert attention! Having captured a mouse a handsome Boobook flies to a bough preparatory to pinching the victim about neck and skull junction. Usually the clutch of talon-shod toes is sufficient to kill the victim.

Opposite: Boobook Owl (Ninox novaseelandiae boobook) *of mid-western Victoria pounces on a mouse which may be seen clutched in the talon-shod toes of its left foot. The eye colour is greyish-green.*

Having crushed the skull and main bones of its mouse victim while holding it in one foot, a Boobook Owl prepares to gulp the meal whole.

Opposite: Boobook Owls—male left, female right.

Three adult and two young Boobook Owls in a typical daylight perch in the foliage of ⌐ silver wattle tree.

Male Boobook Owl relaxing from its slim, stiff, stick-like attitude adopted on the approach of creatures potentially dangerous.

Clutch of Boobook Owl eggs in situ. It usually numbers three, rarely four, and the eggs are rounded.

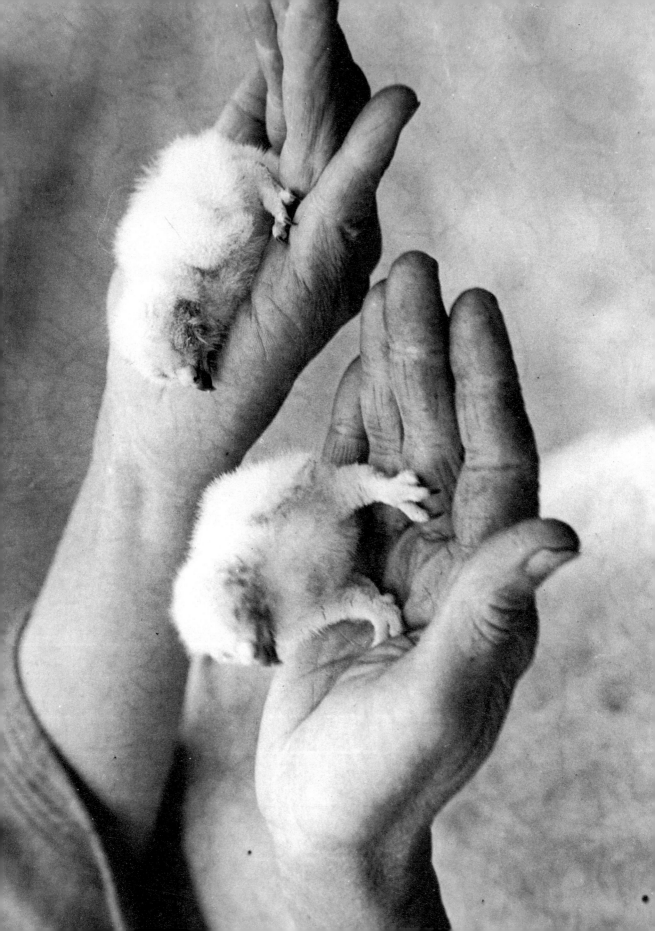

Boobook Owlet: 'At seven weeks, they slept in the wattle tree with their parents'.

Opposite: *Boobook chicks roughly six days old, blind, helpless, but capable of feeble trilling notes; egg-breakers prominent on beaks.*

A Boobook Owlet eight weeks of age is a most appealing little fellow, given to gymnastic head winding, playful ways and a shrill cricket-like trilling.

Children with Boobook Owlets at the nest-leaving stage.

Boobook Owl sunbathing.

Chapter Eight

The Boobook Owls —
Most Versatile of Them All

Without a doubt, Australia's population of Boobook Owls runs into millions for almost anywhere one camps at night, and this includes Tasmania, the leisurely sing-song 'morepork' call is as typical as the very gum trees. The clear characteristic double note (and incidentally all *Ninox* members specialize in a two-syllabled signal),* belongs as much to the clear starlit nights as the laugh of kookaburras and carol of magpies are the familiar bird voices of the days. To the Aborigines it sounded like 'buc-buc' or 'boobook' giving us a very sensible vernacular, but early English colonists, ignorant of the small brown owl (which weighs only 10 to 11 oz.) believed that in this strange new land it was a cuckoo calling by night. It took them years to learn that Aussie cuckoos either whistled or screamed, but did not conform to European standards.

It is by no means an exaggeration to claim that, if there is such a thing as a typically Australian owl, then it is the Boobook which has a great tolerance to all kinds of environment, and occurs in every type of habitat, from dense *Eucalyptus regnans* forests and tropical jungle to the most arid parts of the inland where it camps by day in creek-bed trees, under overhanging rocks and in caves. Naturally, with such a supreme adaptability it is not surprising to find that it occurs in at least sixteen races overflowing the Australian continent, from Tasmania to Timor and Alor, through southern New Guinea to Norfolk Island and New Zealand.

* According to H. L. Bell, *Emu* Vol. 67, Parts 1 and 2, *Ninox theomacha* of New Guinea has a similar but quite distinct call from that of a Boobook.

The New Zealand bird, once classified as distinct from the Australian Boobooks and called Spotted Owl, is retained by Mees (in *A Revision of The Australian Owls,* 1964) as the nominate or original species *(Ninox novaeseelandiae novaeseelandiae),* while all other Boobooks are grouped as forms of it. In passing, it is noteworthy that both the New Zealand and closely similar Tasmanian birds are not only smaller and darker, but exhibit golden-yellow eyes and pale yellow toes as against the grey-green eyes and white toes of mainland Boobooks. The coincidence of yellow to orange eyes among those *Ninox* owls specializing in certain daylight activities may at some time or other be worthy of investigation. I have watched New Zealand 'moreporks' hunting in late afternoon, and of course, a Barking Owl thinks nothing of a diurnal raid.

All these forms of the little Brown Owl, five on the Australian mainland alone (Mees 1964) and variable even in themselves, caused Ernst Mayr at the time of his revision of the northern races, to emphasize that the classification of Boobooks was one of the most difficult problems he had ever encountered, and that variations seemed to be related less to geographical districts, than to rainfall and humidity. 'One therefore encounters not infrequently,' he wrote, 'indistinguishable populations at widely separated localities.'

The Red Boobook *(N. novaeseelandiae lurida)* of Cape York Peninsula, ranging at least as far south as Cardwell, and the Northern Boobook Owl *(N. novaeseelandiae ocellata)* from north-western Australia to north Queensland, are much richer red and much paler respectively than the better known widespread form of Boobook. Generally speaking, then, field observations on appearance, overall hunting habits and calls of all these small, closely related owls are so similar that in writing about one you cover, in all probability, the essentials of all.

The extra small Tasmanian race *(N. novaeseelandiae leucopsis),* strongly spotted beneath, is unique in being partly migratory—some birds visiting the mainland in winter time. With collection dates ranging between April and October, it has proved not uncommon in Victoria, but rare in New South Wales which, as Mees points out, is consistent with winter visits and the time-distance factors.

An injustice of the bird world involving the Boobook Owl persists even today in many parts of Australia. It is the insistent misnomer of 'morepork' for the Tawny Frogmouth because this open-perching master of camouflage, which is not an owl at all, is occasionally found sitting by day in trees from which the Boobook Owl has 'mopoked' the prior night. Again circumstantial evidence gives credit where it is not at all due and so the wrong bird carries the label of 'morepork'.

Even Australian cities provide new 'fields' for conquest as far as the ubiquitous Boobook is concerned, and suburbs of Adelaide, Melbourne, Sydney and Brisbane have their little Brown Owls perching in palms and garden trees, sallying forth after dark to dine easily and richly on the moths and beetles attracted to street lights and also on sparrows and mice, inevitable hangers-on of man's abode.

Last of all owls to nest each season, the rich brown Boobook usually has its fluffy, comical owlets on the wing in early December. This is a delight anticipated here in Queensland each year because we have several pairs of established Boobooks dwelling in the timber of our West Burleigh Fauna Reserve. One favourite spot is located right over the front gate in the highest hollow of a gnarled old spotted gum. Like the home units of many another Gold Coast establishment, this ancient eucalypt is practically 'booked out' with co-tenants ranging from bees to silver-grey possums.

However, the local 'mickies' have decided objections to the presence of owls and frequently during days of the nesting season, live up to their reputation as Noisy Miners by thronging the door-way and hurling the most dreadful abuse at the mother, or mother and babies, deep in the dim interior.

As a child of nine or ten, I fell hard for Boobook owlets away back in the year my parents took me on a short vacation to pretty Lorne on the eastern sea boundary of Victoria's Otway Ranges. The sight of three tiny white ghosts, softly downed, trilling like crickets, and winding their heads round and round in the liveliest manner at the wonder of the night world, enchanted me as nothing ever had before. When after long battles to get there, my earlier journalistic efforts began appearing in the Melbourne *Argus* and *Australasian,* they did so under the *nom-de-plume* of 'Boobook'.

One of the very first of these owls I encountered in juvenile days flitted occasionally after dark about our garden in Ballarat, Victoria. Evidently it ran a pick-up service, much to the detriment of local mice. I well remember the flash of inspiration that suggested the nocturnal visitor might be interested enough to come closer, could I but show him one of mother's chickens. Imagine my stupefaction when the brown raider swooped silently towards my feet and passed on, clutching the protesting chick in very sure talons. I never told mother about that missing chick!

As a primary school boy I had a mate named Ken Murray, whose father was Stationmaster at the bush siding of Waubra Junction. There one day we climbed a dead peppermint and in the top-most hollow found two delightful baby Boobooks. Later we discovered another nest, and in 1924 ideas blossomed for setting them up and observing their behaviour at close range.

That year my parents attended an ANZAAS science congress in Brisbane and, greatly daring, I withdrew everything to my credit in the bank (twenty-four pounds) and 'blew' the lot in purchasing some very long oregon four-by-twos and a quarter-plate Graflex camera. In spite of inevitable retribution in the shape of a thrift-conscious father, the move turned out a good one. I learned carpentering the hard way, in dawn and evening hours, by enclosing a living apple tree, a dead pine tree, and part of a silver wattle tree in a wire netted enclosure sixteen feet high, thirty-three feet long, and thirteen feet wide. I saved one end's work and half of a long side by coming in against a paling boundary fence and the lavatory.

So now the Boobooks owned a lovely home and just to hear the chorus of calling at night was entertainment such as I had never known. Bushland was on my doorstep and through the portals of the owl sanctuary I entered an 'Alice in Wonderland' world of fascination and delight.

Each day I managed to trap odd sparrows upon which dead prey, with occasional mice, the owls waxed in health and vigour. It soon became apparent to me that to live for any length of time they needed natural prey such as small birds, mammals and insects, so that pellets of bone, fur and wing cases could be constantly ejected. I found that, if kept for any time without this food and living on raw meat alone, the owls rectified matters by swallowing small quantities of bark—this action giving rise once more to the usual ejection of pellets, though naturally of a different consistency. To watch an owl preparing to disgorge one of these small objects is always entertaining. His eyes take on an expression which is distinctly oriental; he yawns repeatedly and finally loses the small object containing perhaps the finely-broken bones from the sparrow upon which he made his last meal. Sometimes the pellet is disgorged into the receptive grip of talons and drowsily inspected before final rejection.

88

The dead pine tree served the owls as a dark, warm retreat during the cold months of Ballarat, for the winter is quite severe on that elevated southern plateau. In summertime the birds usually drowsed through the days in the boughs of the silver wattle. Although there were several log shells and boxes arranged after the manner of the hollows in old bush trees high up in the enclosure, I never knew the birds to frequent such hideaway spots during daylight, except of course, in the breeding season. Even in bitter weather they preferred always to perch in a tree of moderate foliage. Very often in that district I found this species of owl spending the day in branches of the pretty native cherry trees *(Exocarpus)*—also taking advantage of the plantations of introduced pines.

Naturally, unlike the Barn or Delicate Owl, the coloration of the hardy Boobook's plumage lends itself to an inconspicuous open life, and again the Boobook, like the Barking Owl, has a protective attitude which, though not nearly so wonderful as that of the Frogmouth, is somewhat similar.

On the approach of danger the owl draws itself up rigidly, the feathers contract closely to the body, the incomplete facial disc shrinks—the bird turns side on to the intruder and you may well imagine that a slim brown stick is regarding you from the spot previously occupied by a Boobook Owl. Several times I have endeavoured to photograph this position but on each occasion the birds have discarded it too soon. On one occasion I saw them assume it on the approach of a gaily dressed lady. Not being used to such arresting spectacles, they obviously considered that danger approached.

The Boobook Owl, or for that matter, any species of owl which makes itself conspicuous by movement during daytime, is usually unmercifully mobbed by smaller birds, and about Ballarat one of the most daring attackers is the White-eared Honeyeater. Of course on the wide plains with their lack of thickets and only occasional hollow trees, the Boobook Owl is forced to make the latter his habitation so that the birds are flushed from such positions when an observer clambers up the right tree trunk. In forest country, on the other hand, when Boobook Owls sleep in such trees as the native cherry they are not always seen, because the mere appearance of an intruder suffices for silent departure to a safer haven.

Sometimes the enclosure occupied by these early owls of mine was visited by young and foolish sparrows and starlings, but no sooner did any of these unfortunates squeeze through the one and a half inch netting than a brown flash, with the apparent speed of lightning and noiselessness of night, seized its victim in sure talons— carrying the unfortunate to a convenient bough where the spine, at neck and skull junction, was broken, the body semi-plucked and usually deposited in a convenient hide for further use. The parents of such luckless youngsters created a most distressing clamour and I was usually aware of what was going on. Starlings however, were not relished and, as a rule, the owls did little more than kill them.

The judgment and skill of the Boobook Owl in capturing night-flying moths and insects are admirable.

Either day or night, I had but to throw the body of a mouse high into the air to observe similar tactics. One or two of the five owls would sally swiftly forth either grasping the mouse in his talons as it fell, or turning completely upside down intercepting the rodent before it reached the ground, to return gracefully to a perch.

Each day at dawn most, if not all, of the owls indulged in a bath, seeming thoroughly to enjoy it even in the coldest of weather. I even knew them, when fluttering vigorously in water, to give vent to shrill wavering screams of excitement.

Of the five adults in the enclosure, two were females and the other three male birds. The females of these examples of the southern mainland race *(Ninox novaeseelandiae boobook)* appeared slightly larger and sturdier than the males, but the plumage of the sexes was much alike, and each individual bird was characterized by a different mottling and varied fulvous striations of the under-surface. In other words, the great variation characterizing individuals among Boobook Owls, which has given rise to endless confusion, puzzled me even in those early days. Also, following the summer moult each owl donned mottling which appeared to me not precisely that of the previous season. As far as I could tell (with the probable bias of young enthusiasm), those lovely birds were even more handsome year by year and whereas here the irides of the male birds' eyes were greyish in tint, those of the females appeared quite green.

In the wild state young Boobook Owls are generally hatched from the eggs (two to three, rarely four) during November, and there is but the single brood of two or three owlets per year, though occasionally some untoward accident causes the parent birds to rear a late brood. The young owls lose their downy breasts and general fluffy appearance completely at the age of three months, when the mottled brown plumage takes its place. Young male birds in Victoria are characterized from perhaps three weeks of age by a lightness of plumage, whereas young females are darker.

The voice of the baby owl is a gentle, high-pitched trilling whistle and this is retained until the bird reaches the age of nearly five months. The voice then deepens and becomes a trilling call of much lower tone. The young owl is capable now of giving vent to the peculiar rapid staccato notes which resemble a succession of 'por-por-por-pors' or 'mor-mor-mor-mors', just as it strikes the fancy. The sub-adult birds utter also a much more leisurely 'hoo! hoo! hoo!' which develops as they become older into a sharp well defined 'wow-wow-wow' or 'yow! yow! yow!' This peculiar cat-like cry broadcast through an open beak is given eight or nine times rapidly in a session by the bird, especially during autumn and winter. It is quite striking, corresponds to the Barking Owl's scream and appears more frequently used by the female birds. I have always associated this cry with Ballarat's freezing winter nights building up for the stinging white frosts of morning.

Finally late in July the young birds of the prior season begin for the first time to use the 'morepork' call. In the wild, of course, they may give vent to the cry earlier, but I never knew my birds to do so. This period is prior, of course, to the pairing season of August and September. Whereas from July onwards the young birds commence their characteristic nocturnal 'morepork' calls, the adult birds, one and all, redouble their vocal efforts; this applies particularly to the males. Here another point arises concerning the 'mopoke' cry. In every case I have had under observation, the male's double call has been clearer and shorter than the leisurely notes of the female. Prior to the mating season the female owl called regularly at different times of the night in answer to the male bird and her voice was uttered in lower key. It seemed more deliberate and expressive—you might almost describe it as a hoarser call, but each individual owl had a style of its own in the nocturnal concert period, and listening to Boobooks when camped in the wilds, I have usually thought that I could distinguish between calls of a male and female. Once again, as apparently in all *Ninox* owls, the double call is a closed-beak performance.

At this same period of those charming old Ballarat days, a dilapidated female Boobook was brought along for much-needed care and attention. Having been kept in a small cage for many months, the unfortunate bird had injured its upper beak by continual beating at night against its cage wire. Not long after I received it the upper beak broke off below the nostrils, and only by the patient process of feeding the unfortunate on tiny pieces of meat small enough for immediate swallowing, did it slowly recover strength and grow a new beak.

In 1925, one of the male birds which had lost its mate the season before courted and paired off with this hen owl. Immediately on nightfall throughout the month of August, he would fly to a branch near the hen bird and start softly on the 'por-por-por' notes. Without exaggeration he could maintain this in monotonous staccato fashion for two and three hundred repetitions—sometimes raising the tone sharply or dropping back into the quiet monotone. Then the female bird would sidle up to him, fondle his feathers gently, and call repeatedly in the trilling low-toned rumble. Following this the male Boobook usually raised his voice, and sitting beside his new mate, called 'morepork-morepork-morepork' in a voice vibrating with excitement.

Each night at moonrise there came a regular chorus from the birds, and often at this time I would see a pair of visiting owls float noiselessly overhead to perch in a near-by tree, adding a staccato chorus of greeting 'por-pors' to the already loud chorus of 'morepork'.

Fascinating calls of those early Boobooks flooded back one velvety night of half moon and clear winking stars, not so long ago, under the skimpy roof of a bush saw mill near Kin Kin in Queensland. Two of the small brown owls flew to a roof beam, whence the male serenaded his mate endlessly, unaware that his 'entertainment' evoked fond memories in an observer who happened to be me, awakened from sleep on a sawdust bed below.

During the pre-nesting period the Ballarat male Boobook gave vent to another note, or rather to that which is in reality a rousing cry. Strictly speaking it is a projection of the trilling low-toned note which the owls usually make use of among themselves, and to me as a friend, emitted in a rising high-pitched tone with greater volume. It is quite distinct from the small shrill scream given by two of the birds, which may be quarrelling over a sparrow or a mouse, or used again when a Boobook Owl is trapped or restrained. This particular cry is used in a similar though modified shrill

Opposite: *The Boobook is a rich brown owl, usually with grey-green eyes, contrasting with the yellow eyes and greyish plumage of the Barking Owl.*

Adult Frogmouth (left), a grey bird, contrasted with adult male Boobook Owl (right), a brown bird. Confusion over call notes has led to the erroneous label of Mopoke for the Frogmouth. The true Mopoke is the Boobook Owl.

Male Boobook flies down in daylight and drops food in front of his owlets.

fashion by fledgeling Boobook Owls when hungry.

The site picked by the two owls for a nursery was one of the boxes which I had arranged high up after the manner of a high class tree hollow—the floor being littered with bark as I had seen in odd nurseries of Boobook Owls in the bush situated in hollows and spouts, heavily padded with ancient flattened nests of ring-tailed possums. From the middle of September the male owl frequented this man-made hollow each night. He usually flew straight in at dusk and the 'por-por-por' notes would be heard issuing in muffled tones. The female sometimes flew in also, but the work of preparing the hollow for eggs was done almost exclusively by the cock bird. With the aid of his strong talons and sharp hooked beak he tore and shredded the bark into soft fibrous material—then lying flat he would scrape rapidly with alternate feet, creating a clear bare space which met with approving 'por-pors' from the hen. Each night the scratching sound was clearly audible as the owl industriously repeated his performance.

The female bird took to the nest on 27 September and from then on she passed the day in the hollow. Her first egg was laid on 30 September and the next appeared, I think, two days later. Of the exact interval I am not sure, but she sat closely from the beginning on the comparatively large, rounded eggs in her comfortable home and was very attentively looked after not only by her mate, but by the three other owls living in the enclosure. During daylight the male bird often flew up to the hollow with a sparrow in his talons, leaving it there for the use of his brooding mate. Strangely enough, the other female owl showed every inclination of helping the sitting bird in the process of brooding. This proved most fortunate, for nine days from the inception of incubatory duties the sitting owl suddenly became ill. She left the hollow and fell to the ground below. Fortunately the sickness proved but a passing phase, though at the time I thought all hope was lost. Some two or three hours passed and during this time the other female covered the deserted eggs very capably and saved them from probable disaster. This opportune act obviously retrieved the situation and eventually the owner of the eggs resumed her brooding and suffered no return of the unfortunate illness. The male bird and his three companions continued to feed her constantly and regularly with moths, raw

Opposite: *Compare the rich brown plumage of this Boobook Owl with the more greyish hues of the Barking Owl.*

meat, mice and sparrows. She sat on steadily—the only time, as far as I know, that she left the hollow being just at dusk and, on the average, she stayed away from the eggs as long as half an hour. On warm nights she indulged in a flutter bath.

A fortnight passed and during this time a second pair of the owls, which had been courting for some time, prepared another hollow and the female, the same bird which had saved the eggs during the illness of number one breeding owl, commenced brooding on two round white eggs of her own. You will gather from this that territory consciousness—so very pronounced in Powerful Owls and well developed to an extent also in the Barking Owl, is not so obvious in Boobook Owls—meaning that pairs may nest comparatively close to one another, as in our sixty-five acre Queensland Fauna Reserve where some three lots share this comparatively small area of bushland. A pair of Powerful Owls 'owning' twice this area would have guarded it fiercely against any other Powerful Owl.

In the Boobooks' aviary the new arrangement left an odd male bird out—but, remarkable to relate, he was as attentive as either of the other cock birds in looking after both sitting owls. They called 'morepork' very often at night and occasionally gave vent to the cry in broad daylight following the capture of a sparrow. Obviously this was sheer delight following a victorious sally. Again at night they gave long effusions of the staccato 'por-por-por' notes, and on taking a moth or other insect into either of the hollows, were received by the sitting owl with slow deliberate 'por-pors' of appreciation, for in this call again the female is more deliberate.

Three weeks passed and being a novice at breeding these birds I was disappointed. It seemed that after all no young birds would hatch from the eggs of owl number one who had been brooding for that particular time. However, she sat on contentedly, leaving her treasures each evening for the mere regulation half hour.

By the time four weeks had passed only the fact of normal behaviour on the part of the birds prevented me from abandoning all hope. Then on 1 November, thirty-three days from the laying of the first egg, two very small owlets were hatched. They were blind, covered with white down, and carried prominent egg breakers on the tiny hook-shaped beaks. Naturally it was a day of great triumph. We had bred our wonderful Boobook Owls for the first time and, as far as could be ascertained, it was also a first record.

From this moment on, for a whole week, the mother owl apparently stuck fast to keeping the babies covered. Not once was

94

she seen outside the hollow. She nursed the little fellows the whole of the time while the other owls supplied her with moths and other dainty owl food.

Most remarkable to relate, it was found that when the other brooding female quitted her clutch each evening, she found time to be as industrious as any of the other owls in collecting items for the new-hatched babies. I am afraid that their arrival upset her own chances of bringing out youngsters, for each night she spent more and more time away from her eggs, devoting it to the service of the first owl's offspring. Sufficient to say that after brooding in this interrupted fashion for five weeks and a few days, she suddenly deserted her clutch forever, becoming as much the owner and protector of the owlets as the actual mother herself. On breaking the unsuccessful eggs, I found one dead youngster right at the hatching stage, and an embryo chick in the second egg, dead at development of perhaps a fortnight.

When photographing the young owls at the age of seven days I was staggered at the collection of moths, beetles and other food which had been stacked in a corner of the nursery.

From the day of hatching, the owlets were capable of feeble trilling notes and when handled at the age of seven days they made instinctive attempts to receive food from one's fingers, presuming, though still blind, that their parents were awakening them for a meal. The downy white chicks were treasured by all adult birds and woe betide an intruder. A tame ring-tailed possum in the habit of promenading by night about the high framework of the enclosure with her youngsters was now savagely attacked by the owls below, and she wisely gave up her gambles in that particular direction.

The female owls, which prior to the nesting season were remarkably tame, now attacked me unmercifully whenever I climbed to the hollow in order to photograph the owlets. One would sweep up behind me, knocking off my hat with a blow from her talons, and occasionally the other owl followed suit, raking my bare head cruelly with her sharp claws. As long as I remained in the vicinity these birds continued to attack, and besides receiving quite painful wounds, I had a felt hat absolutely ruined. The male bird was quite indifferent, leaving the protection of the youngsters to the larger and sturdier hen birds.

This reminds me of an episode of later years when I happened to walk by night beneath a large hollow tree near Torquay, Victoria.

My hat was struck from my head by a Boobook Owl, which swept up to its launching tree again, winding its head about and watching me intently. I discovered the hard way how very daring and wholehearted these small owls may be in the care of their young ones. On the other hand, they are also fond of fun and mischief. On a number of occasions, I witnessed visiting Boobooks in the garden at night knocking roosting Magpies out of the trees, swooping on the terrified birds as they ran along the ground, and glaring at them with huge eyes in bristling heads revolving on 'rubber' necks.

As is the way with the species, the young owls developed quite slowly and at the age of fifteen days they were still quite helpless, though their eyes had opened. The mother bird and her helpful female assistant remained in the hollow with them all day, sallying forth at dusk to hunt industriously for food. The male birds were just as energetic, the result being that almost every morsel of food collected was taken into the hollow and the adult birds retained little for themselves.

Whenever I went, with some trepidation, up the ladder to the hollow the females emerged quickly, snapping their beaks and glaring anxiously and angrily at me from near-by branches. Then would come the attack. I wondered whether the two birds would ever resume their quiet trusting ways with me again, for nothing delighted one of them more in the pre-nesting time than to perch on my shoulder after dark and converse in softly uttered 'por-pors'.

The male owl always watched me at the nursery, but remained consistently neutral, never thinking of resenting my presence nor of being unpleasant in any way.

The baby owls continued to thrive and grow and had an indescribable, but attractive, odour of their own. At nineteen days I was in the act of photographing them when the male parent flew down with a mouse in his beak and dropped it in front of the owlets. Thus I was able to obtain a most interesting picture. At twenty-four days of age the youngsters showed distinct advancement, the small wings boasting a showing of faintly-spotted brown feathers, while the owlets were becoming distrustful and even defiant of the camera. Each night now their two white heads, with ghost-like movements, peered from the entrance to the dark hollow, filled with wonder at the greatness of the world. They wound their heads in all directions and surveyed the scenery from every conceivable angle.

A month from the time of hatching they showed strong resentment at being handled and clapped their beaks vigorously whenever I touched them. They assumed most dignified positions and made tremendous eyes in their own quaint fashion. Their trilling whistles were continuous at night, and from dusk onwards the old birds worked busily floating back and forth like great moths in the silvery moonlight of early December.

From the five weeks stage onwards the young birds proved far more venturesome, and on 12 December they fluttered from the hollow for the very first time, being then forty-three days or roughly six weeks old. I recollect the worry of the mother owl when the fluffy youngsters flew unsteadily across the enclosure, hanging for five minutes or more upside down on the wire netting, apparently wondering why they could go no further. The mother used all her wiles to coax the little ones back again to the nursery, finally succeeding, but whilst they were out she sat beside each one in turn, jealously guarding them against possible danger.

Though Boobook Owls are remarkably active at dusk and again at dawn, I have noted that on dark nights during cloud overcast or absence of the moon they are very quiet, and like other species of *Ninox* remain perched in one position for hours at a time. Visiting owls in the garden did exactly the same thing.

The female parent owl and her faithful companion left the young ones to their own devices during daylight from the age of nineteen days, sleeping as formerly in the branches of the wattle tree, but keeping the hollow under strict observation. As often as not, the owlets perched on prey such as sparrows left in the hollow over the daylight period, waiting for the parents to arrive at dusk so that the items could be torn asunder for their benefit.

From the time of leaving the hollow for the first time the young owls appeared each night winding their pretty heads round and about at everything, and especially at the flickering shadows cast from the hurricane lantern I carried. They occasionally turned their heads so far round that their beak points faced skywards. They believed strongly in taking stock of the world from every conceivable angle and often indulged in the exercise of flapping their wings until they resembled small whirlwinds—trilling excitedly all the while. With the return of daylight they retired to the hollow once more, but a significant stage was reached at the age of seven weeks, when they deserted the nursery entirely and perched with their parents in the wattle tree throughout succeeding days.

The old birds now gave them mice, sparrows etc. whole, and it was entertaining to watch the youngsters holding these unfortunates in their talons, showing every sign of contentment and now and again beaking the victims in an amateurish way. They also wound their heads round and round at the prey in drowsy fashion and when finally plucking the item, would eat all the feathers instead of discarding them.

The Boobook Owl occasionally preys upon frogs, but these are not popular items, and I think that only extremely poor conditions in winter time would see the acceptance of such poor fare as these lowly and distasteful amphibians.

Another peculiarity of the young owls in their indecisive tackling of prey was their method of approach. Instead of commencing on the head of a sparrow and holding the victim firmly under the talons, the young owls invariably started anywhere and had a most difficult and prolonged task in disposing of their early suppers.

In much more recent times here in Queensland, a Boobook Owl brought to mind the fact that a powerful maternal instinct, aroused by the appeal of young and helpless creatures, is not the prerogative of man alone. Hard-hearted cuckoos trade upon the mother love of other birds, and strangely assorted foster-parent-children associations hit the headlines from time to time. However, this particular case concerning two Barking Owlets, 'Hughie' and 'Little Mattie', was surely one of the strangest, since it involved a wild would-be mother Boobook of a species different from their own.

Going out to feed these lively, trilling twins from Gin Gin as I habitually did each evening in the days of their infancy, I noticed my small, yellow dog Dot leaping up at intervals in the moonlight, barking frustratedly the while. Closer observation revealed a swift black shadow skimming within inches of the indignant dog each time she approached the Barking Owl aviary. Fox-like in colour and appearance, she was under attack by an indignant Boobook Owl. Its base for sorties was an overhanging Moreton Bay fig where, fiery-eyed in the spotlight, the bird was revealed as an 'elderly female' of old acquaintance. Now the trilling baby calls of Barking Owls are quite reminiscent, though not nearly so shrill, as those of infant Boobook Owls and under the misapprehension that these were some of her own kind the old Boobook had obviously appointed herself guardian of the Barking Owl youngsters. All day for quite a time, she camped in the nearest protective shrubbery, necessarily keeping a weather eye lifting, for such shelter was far from adequate as a protection against the heckling of Mickies and Butcher-birds.

By night she collected tender 'small calibre' rats and sat dutifully overhead. Some of her delicacies with thoughtfully broken bones were left in an old Peewee nest by the cage roof, and these I was only too glad to hand on. Saddest aspect of all this devotion and self sacrifice on the part of the little brown 'mother', was the complete lack of appreciation on the part of both Little Mattie and Hughie. They responded instantly to human talk but never to the language of that poor, persistent, well meaning, little Boobook Owl.

An interesting appendix to the Hawk Owl group lies in a table of clutch number per species and individual egg measurements (after H. G. Barnard for the Rufous Owl, N. J. Favaloro for the southern Powerful Owl, and M. T. Goddard for the remainder).
Boobook Owl *(Ninox novaeseelandiae boobook)*
 41 × 36.5 mms.
 41 × 36 mms.
 40.5 × 36 mms.   Tenterfield, N.S.W.
Barking Owl *(Ninox connivens connivens)*
 47 × 39 mms.
 47.5 × 39.5 mms.   Grafton, N.S.W.
Rufous Owl *(Ninox rufa marginata)*
 53 × 44.5 mms.
 54.5 × 44.5 mms.   Cardwell, Q.
Powerful Owl *(Ninox strenua)*
 51.1 × 43.4 mms.   Type set
 49.0 × 43.2 mms.   Mt Riddell, Victoria.
Powerful Owl *(Ninox strenua)*
 56 × 45 mms.
 55 × 46 mms.
 56 × 46 mms.
 54 × 45.5 mms.
 54 × 45.5 mms.   north-eastern N.S.W.
 53.5 × 46 mms.   (Clarence River tributaries).

The interesting fact emerges that the set of Rufous Owl eggs is superior in individual size to those of the type clutch of Powerful Owl eggs from Mt Riddell, Victoria, whereas in measurement eggs of Powerful Owls from north-eastern New South Wales exceed them both.

Chapter Nine

Masked or Monkey-faced Owls — the Barn Owl (Ghost Bird)

Very conveniently from the point of view of identification and discussion, Nature provided Australia with two wonderfully well defined groups—or, more strictly speaking, families—of owls: the fore-running Hawk Owls (Strigidae) and the now more stereo-typed Masked Owls (Tytonidae). In these days of television thrillers the children might very well refer to the latter bunch as the masked bandits, and not be far out at that! The heart-shaped facial disc, like a giant radio telescope, is thought to be an aid in detecting sound waves from not-so-near quarry, enabling quick perception of squeaking rats and mice which might otherwise be so easily by-passed.

In all probability, these owls are the symbols of wisdom that gave rise to such verse as Tennyson's:

'Alone and warming his five wits
The White owl in the belfry sits',

and the anonymous:

'Twas a wise old owl who lived in an oak
Who the more he saw the less he spoke
But the less he spoke the more he heard
Why can't we be like that wise old bird?'

At one time or another, most country dwellers have glimpsed the whitish, ghostly Barn Owl, smallest, most widespread, most active and most numerous of these 'monkey-faced' birds. Fond of perching by night on fence posts and tree stumps, it is an absolute wizard at dropping stone-like in flight with clutching talons upon foraging mice in the grasslands.

The co-ordination between hearing and action in a dim light, or in no light at all, which is such a feature of the Barn Owl, is one of

Remarkable bluff of the Barn Owl. These antics of swaying wing-spread action with snapping beak, hisses and a fierce glare were triggered by the presence of a possum above the camera lens.

Dudley McMillan on rope ladder marks the approximate position of the inside Barn Owl nursery in the old forest red gum outside Burleigh Drive-In Theatre. The tree was specially spared by Queensland Main Roads Dept during new road construction.

The ghostly Barn Owl is a beautiful bird invaluable as a check on rats and mice. It is also notable for its prolific reproduction and vulnerability to shortages in food supply. A characteristic post-sitting attitude.

Established home of Barn Owls at entrance gateway of Burleigh Drive-In Picture Theatre, Gold Coast, Queensland. The tree is a venerable forest red gum and the site, entered from above, is indicated by Dudley McMillan's tomahawk.

Steps and stairs! Australian Barn Owls brood up to seven eggs in a clutch, sitting from the time of appearance of Number One. Hence the disparity or gradation in size between the eldest (18 days) and youngest (11 days), of these quadruplets.

Twenty-five day old eldest Barn Owlet (centre) and its younger brood members, showing the signs of coming beauty as they lose their long 'miserable' faces.

Barn Owlet twins approximately twenty-five days old—the 'powderpuff' stage.

its fascinating facets and I recall that American researchers experimented with this bird in dark, totally enclosed rooms with deadened walls.

Using hidden watching devices, they have released individual mice inside on a spread of leaves to find the hungry owl instantly overhead, hovering head down, with the disc-like feather arrangement of the face acting as a large 'ear'. Sure of its strike, the owl throws up its wings and drops with talons spread wide so that they lie in the path of hearing and avoid parallax error from the difference in position between feet and ears.

In spite of the fact that the mouse under these conditions is scarcely a clattering horse, one grab was usually enough to procure a certain meal. Obviously the Ghost Bird is sensitively equipped for its specialized life hunting small wide-awake rodents.

Just as the Boobook outnumbers all Australian Hawk Owls, so correspondingly among Masked Owls can the Barn Owl lay claim to being the most widespread and numerous, having spread to Tasmania also.

Male and female are much of a size, with the female often a shade larger. Differently shaped from the Boobook, the Barn Owl is slightly bigger (14–16 oz.) and stands higher. It is a bird of beautiful plumage with the real owl face—the well-defined disc characteristic of the 'wise old owl' of childhood story books. An alias of 'Delicate Owl' applies equally as readily to the infinite loveliness of its feathering, as it does to the occasional winter death that thins its numbers.

No photograph or description can do real justice to the harmony of delicate beauty in the Barn Owl's appearance. Back and wings are brownish-grey inclining to yellow, spotted with black, brown and white markings, while the under surface is white, dotted with a varying number of brownish spots. While younger owls are heavily spotted here some adults are almost pure white.

So conspicuous indeed in daylight is the Barn Owl that the need for shelter inside a tree trunk is immediately apparent. Several times I have known magpies and kookaburras to kill inexperienced owlets of this kind, mercilessly exposed in sunlight, where they stand out more obviously than a grand final footballer bereft of his togs.

However, daylight perching in dense vegetation, in rocky shelters, in stands of river sheokes and dark forests of exotic pines, are by no means uncommon. On such occasions the Barn Owl's 'shrivelled' appearance, due to a positive shrinking of the facial disc and clever covering of most of the body by the wings, renders it much at one with the environment.

Dumping odds and ends into his rubbish receptacle one morning in May 1960, Mr L. Giovine of Riverside Drive, Surfers' Paradise, Queensland was startled to find an exceptionally blonde Barn Owl watching him from the shadow of the bin. Weak and almost flightless, the bird proved to be a grounded youngster with just enough down to indicate recent departure from the nest, but if ever there was a rare white specimen of this always light-coloured owl, here indeed was that one. An immaculate snowy body and pleated facial disc were only faintly relieved by a yellowish tinge on wings and back, and by pink legs. Naturally the remarkable apparition was immediately christened 'Spook' the phantom.

In sunlight, which naturally he disliked intensely, Spook's plumage was dazzling, and it was obvious that because of his very conspicuousness, interfering Mickies, Butcher Birds and Magpie Larks had hounded the ghostly fellow from trees to earth. At all events, following nights of gorging on tender mice and luscious baby rats, Spook was back in business and snapped his beak warningly at any intrusion upon his privacy. He was a beautiful and most unusual specimen of his kind—a snow-white even amongst his pale, normally-patterned relatives.

My very first meeting with the Barn Owl ended in tragedy of a kind that induced months of regret and self-recrimination. It was spring 1923, and as a schoolboy on a lone Saturday cycle trip to Lake Learmonth beyond Ballarat, Victoria, I climbed a hollow tree standing alone on those lightly timbered basalt plains. Because of the trunk scratches I expected to find a possum, but instead, out from a hole above my head flew a nearly white owl. Peering in, I saw, to my intense delight a single, swaying, beak-snapping owlet which I thought one of the most wonderful and attractive birds I had met. Reaching in at a dangerous angle, and never minding the talon stabs and beak tearing in those exciting moments, I got the baby out, took its picture, and later made it comfortable in a sugar bag for the long ride home.

I have always hated even to recall the long ago return trip, but what happened, like other accidents, cannot be undone. In those days little bitumen existed, and while negotiating a very rough stretch of road, almost back to base, the carefully nursed bag swung down from the handle bars and became caught in the front wheel.

In a flash it was dragged through the bicycle fork, killing that lovely bird instantly.

Moth-like in its silent flitting appearances, the wraith that is the Barn Owl happens to be one of the most successful colonizers the world has known. Despite a delicate physique which is particularly intolerant of any prolonged period of food shortage, this soft-winged, fly-by-night crossed our coastline long before it was sighted by William Dampier, Captain Cook, or any other of the early navigators, and doubtless stragglers still do arrive.

The name Barn Owl for these rodent specialists originated in England, where the cosmopolitan birds find it convenient to perch in farm buildings handily situated to the rats and mice often numerous in such places.

Flourishing on the American continent, in Europe and Asia, it is considered (Mayr, 1944) that our Australian race of Barn Owl (*Tyto alba delicatula*) arrived originally from India through the Malay Peninsula, Java and the lesser Sunda Islands, and that from Australia it expanded into eastern New Guinea, Polynesia and Melanesia. The reason that such a far-from-robust creature, so specialized in diet, exists, and in large numbers, over such a wide area, is best illustrated by a few experiences.

In 1959 I reared three hen Barn Owls from infancy after their kidnapping from a forest red gum spout on the Mudgeeraba roadside at Burleigh Heads, Queensland. They did not lack a plentiful supply of fat mice and consequently flourished in growth and first-class health.

With the arrival of the month of April and at the age of a mere 11 months, all three owls, without the stimulus of any male bird, retired to a hollow log and laid eggs.★ Accompanied by much fuss and a good deal of nocturnal shrieking, each contributed up to seven in a clutch and sat cheek by jowl, or even one upon the other, in a determined effort to hatch those treasures. Almost as fast as I took the eggs away the birds laid more, so that at the end of two months more than fifty eggs had appeared. Altogether they persisted in these abortive efforts for a good four months.

Now, in April 1967, a mated pair of the birds is setting up house in what we usually regard as the normal nesting time for Barn Owls, but these birds—situated in a suitable aviary with nesting hollow and good food—have nested over the *whole* year from

★ A young mated female at West Burleigh eclipsed this effort on 31 July by laying the first of her eggs at the age of ten months.

April 1966. The expected clutch of eggs, numbering probably five to seven, like its predecessors, will be the eighth consecutive lot in twelve months. The fecundity and persistence of this species in nesting under suitable conditions is unparalleled among Australian or any other owls.

All successfully reared owlets, incidentally, have been released at the self-reliant age of four months, some bearing identification rings affixed by official C.S.I.R.O. bird bander, Mr J. S. Robertson of Wellington Point.

Then away back in May 1928, I have never forgotten fascinating nights sitting about a campfire in the yellow box Stony Rises country of Smeaton, Victoria watching the Barn Owls that had come from near and far to feast on a plague of mice. The calm silence of the starry evenings was broken by the 'sk-air!' 'skee-air!' cries of the mysterious white birds as they floated in all directions over the circle of fire-light and dived into the shadowy trees beyond. Everything, including the fixtures of a near-by bee keeper's hut, smelt atrociously of the millions of mice. So ravenous were these little wretches that on the first night out I had skin chewed off my fingers while I slept.

Incidentally, recurrent reports of mice in plague numbers on the Queensland Darling Downs, as so often happens also in winter time, emphasize again and again the enormous damage done by these little rodents. Unity is colossal strength, when all those tiny incisors gnaw with single-minded purpose into precious bags of grain. Strangely not many people know that the small troublesome villains are our associate colonizers, and not original Australians at all. They are European house mice *(Mus musculus)* which cannot resist the fiesta times of good seasons in this new and roomy land. But what can be more efficient in their control than an aerial patrol working by night, with otherwise hidden rats and mice being picked up when they least expect it? Thus, if you wish to encourage the unpaid services of the economically invaluable Barn Owls, *never destroy the big old trees.* Without the roomy hollow gums so often demolished in 'burning off', the birds cannot remain in the vicinity and their indispensable services are lost for ever.

It has been proved in Europe that in one area in one year, owls take 23,980 rodents per square mile, while authoritative sources claim that in a single night a Barn Owl may capture as much small prey as a dozen cats.

At any rate, the plentiful food supply and numerous hollow

gums of Stony Rises, Victoria back in the good old days of 1928, provided such ideal conditions that the owls were nesting in almost every suitable tree hole. There were families all over the place and the plaintive 'air-sh!' of owlets awaiting their meal of mice was a night-long chorus. Like tiny ghosts they peered down from dark doorways of their nurseries, about which there was absolutely no territorial aggressiveness among parent birds. As usual, every nesting hollow was thickly carpeted with disgorged fur-wrapped pellets of tiny bones and skulls, for, here again, Nature's unbeatable arrangement for the casting out of indigestible material gives these owls, as indeed all others, the maximum nourishment from available food. Pellets of all masked fellows, however, are readily distinguished from those of the *Ninox* Hawk Owls by the sealed and glazed appearance caused by drying out of a strong mucous covering.

In any event, as all good things eventually come to an end, so the flourishing state of affairs on Stony Rises could not last for ever. With the decline and fall of the mouse empire, hastened in onset by lack of food, cold weather and cannibalism, the economy of the Barn Owls was completely upset. By late June that year most of them had dispersed, with a classical example of large numbers of deaths amongst the remnant. According to our discoveries at the time, the majority of defunct owls were immature birds in an emaciated starving state too weak to help themselves.

This winter death among Barn Owls is a well-known phenomenon frequently mentioned in nature columns throughout the world. In the main it is attributed to disease, but after catering for these birds in captivity continuously since the late 1920s, having dead birds post-mortemed without positive results, and watching the development of youngsters, I am convinced that the mortality amongst these prolific birds is a direct result of food shortage, frequently accentuated by the bitter cold of winter periods. Additionally, as emphasized, Barn Owls are predominantly rodent eaters unable to make a ready switch to an alternative diet. Harking back to the previously mentioned mechanics of digestion, it can be said that when a Barn Owl, or any owl for that matter, catches a mouse it does not take it home for a laborious process of skinning, cleaning and cooking prior to a leisurely repast. There is neither time nor need for this, firstly because the actual hunting is frequently arduous and secondly, nature has endowed these night birds with alimentary processes of magnificent efficiency.

A captured victim is held under the feet on a bough, while the hooked beak tears off portions piece-meal (including bones) until the lot has gone down the hatch. Perhaps seven to nine hours later in its day-time retreat, depending upon the extent and size of the prior supper, the owl yawns widely, looks mighty uncomfortable momentarily and disgorges a neatly packaged parcel of fur-wrapped bones, bits and pieces—minus any single trace of nourishing flesh.

From this it is readily understood that owl pellets, including as they do skulls of rats and mice, provide clues of numbers and species of rodents swallowed, and I am indebted to Mr Jack Woods, Director of the Queensland Museum, and his staff, for the following analyses of casts taken at different times of the year from a great hollow tree inhabited by Barn Owls on the Mudgeeraba road outside the Burleigh Drive-In theatre on Queensland's Gold Coast. In the month of May, for instance, one lot of skeletal material brought down from the hollow by Mr Mervyn Goddard included three skulls of the common (introduced) black rat, two of the eastern swamp rat, one from a probable brown or Norwegian rat (also introduced), two of the climbing banana rats (Melomys), amongst indeterminate small bird crania and rodent body bones, but no trace of small marsupials.

Conversely in the month of July there was a complete absence of the larger introduced rats, but at least eleven specimens of the native banana rat (Melomys) and forty-odd skulls of the common mouse of house and field.

One pouched mouse (Sminthopsis murina?) had been too slow off the mark, while a lizard jawbone was probably that of a leaf-tailed gecko. On nights of poorer hunting, the versatile birds had filled in on an insect diet, for beetle wing cases and evidence of bees or wasps also figured in the remains.

Standing impressively alone across the bitumen from Burleigh Drive-In theatre entrance, the large and venerable forest red gum already mentioned is a focal point of the activities of local Barn Owls and it has figured largely in most of my Queensland contacts with the Ghost Birds.

What marks it off from other eucalypts is the fact that the cosy hollow inside, big enough, by the way, for Merv Goddard to enter and descend some ten feet, meets every requirement of Mr and Mrs Barn Owl who have used it successfully year after year as their parents, and even grandparents, probably did before them.

Nesting events are generally heralded from the night skies before laying time, by the high flying male bird who passes over our West Burleigh Reserve excitedly calling 'shir-r-r!' or 'sh------!' and 'skee-air!' Though I cannot be sure, it seems that he is probably carrying food as he heads home less than half an air mile away.

In the hollow tree itself, usually at the 'front door', courting activities by the male take the form of rapid, oft-repeated, low-voiced, sighing cries or wails—should you so interpret them—uttered at night and even in late afternoon. They sound like 'skurr! skurr! skurr! keer! keer!' with endless squealing or shrieking 'sk-eows', while the female remains very local as egg-laying approaches uttering periodic, plaintive, beseeching cries of 'sk-air', 'sk-air', something like those of an owlet encouraging supplies of food.

Patrolling the grasslands thereabouts night by night for rats and mice the whole year through, these handsome and indeed startling birds have cut short the destructive careers of countless thousands of rodents. Most of these end up in winter months in the appreciative beaks of anything from five to seven fluffy owlets waiting eagerly in the old nursery gum. Sad to say another equally useful pair nesting within 300 yards were deprived of home facilities in an irresponsible burn-off some years before.

In early 1963, however, from the Mudgeeraba direction there began an ominous rumbling, ever increasing as days went by. A new highway was under construction and bulldozers, graders and trucks shook not only the earth but the very air. Friendly landmarks disappeared overnight, smoke arose from heaped-up burning ruin and with relentless purpose, the mechanical monsters headed directly for the tree of the owls—already marked for removal. It was then that Albert Shire engineer (Mr T. E. Peters) and foreman (Mr Jim McCourt) stemmed the impending tragedy and with commendable wisdom granted complete immunity to the big old gum. Past it and round it, erasing lesser trees and moving tons of earth—the monsters roared and raced but never a sign did the old birds give. In the hushed stillness of night when the machines slept below, they flew on hunting forays as if nothing was happening, ever urged on by the beseeching owlets. Though scarcely unaware of the earth-changing events about them, their self-contained flat was as high and as secure as ever. For a time indeed food was easier than it had been for quite a while because of the many dispossessed mice scampering distractedly across cleared spaces that were not there before. So the lovely nocturnal ratters and mousers carried on as usual, patrolling far and wide over the local grasslands in their efficient, unpaid and generally unrecognized 'profession'.

Immediately in front of them is a close and unparalleled view of current drive-in programmes, mostly in colour. Below them hundreds of headlights glare each night, but it makes not the slightest difference, and again and again since, they have become immersed in their normal nesting projects of winter time. At such times, father owl redoubles his efforts and evidence of his extra victims appears in the form of the numerous pellets disgorged on the nursery floor. At times he even flies across the beam of picture projection, though even then not many patrons of the show are aware of the drama of life and death being enacted about them during the hours of their entertainment.

How very different was this nesting site in the stately living eucalypt from one located in a thirty foot high, completely burned out, tree shell at Duck Pond camp on the Miriamvale Road, Queensland. Looking straight down inside from above on an October afternoon in 1963, Eric Zillmann reported one much alive and one very dead Powderpuff Owlet almost at ground level within the 'chimney nursery'. Outside on the ground lay a more advanced, but dead and decomposed, owlet. Apparently the hunting had been extremely poor. Mother owl, who had taken off across country like a large white moth, was quickly overtaken by vociferous blue-winged Kingfishers, Kookaburras, Magpies, Butcher Birds and Mickies. The only place for conspicuous Barn Owls out in daytime is another hollow tree, and this the mother bird found very quickly. It was not until night-time when the quacking of black ducks arose from Duck Pond Swamp where Lily Trotters and Dabchicks associate, that the Ghost Birds re-established the even tenor of their ways.

Winter 1962 was a splendid breeding season for Barn Owls in the Gold Coast area of Queensland. Encouraged by plentiful mice in the paddocks and a prevalence of black rats (Rattus rattus) in our large bulldozed rubbish 'quarry', a pair nested in a hollow grey gum one hundred and fifty yards from it and only fifty yards distant from the dingo run. By spotlight, seven rasping owlets presented a dazzling sight as they took nightly bows, crowded in the doorway of a lofty hollow.

Poor mother and father were forced to work mighty hard to provide at least thirty to forty mice per night, or the equivalent in

All night long ever-hungry Barn Owlets crowd the entrance, rasping incessantly for food items. Parent birds run a continual shuttle service.

Paul Gallagher up a grey gum on West Burleigh Fauna Reserve, holding one of four Barn Owlets from a deep hollow above and to his right.

True beauty supersedes ugliness as Barn Owlets develop: eldest bird eight weeks and ready for departure, with youngest bird a week its junior still well clothed in down.

Barn Owl, hissing, snapping its beak and swaying from side to side, endeavours to intimidate an intruder. Nocturnal mammals approaching the nesting site are threatened likewise.

Exceptionally pale, almost pure white Barn Owl discovered by W. L. Giovine of Surfers Paradise, Queensland. Hounded by Noisy Miners and Butcherbirds, it took refuge on the ground in his garden.

rats, to keep those demanding children growing. Later in the same winter, however, the sad phenomenon of mortality peculiar to the birds became rampant in south-eastern Queensland. There was death again among Barn Owls, and in one fortnight alone we found no less than five corpses within a mile radius of our West Burleigh locality. The grand total, including the many carried off unseen by foxes, must have run into hundreds.

Nesting usually from March and April through to October, the birds lay their white elongated (three to seven) eggs in the roomy hollows already mentioned, preferring lightly timbered country wherever it occurs in Australia and Tasmania. Far more voracious than the Hawk Owls these farmers' friends continually scour crops, haystacks and pastures at night, carrying off not only mice and rats but small rabbits as well.

Four of their powderpuff owlets gave us quite a time following a day in May 1960, when Dudley McMillan climbed another big tree near Burleigh and lowered them in a make-shift sling. The removal was carried out under permit, for of course all owls, being useful birds, are strictly protected. Excepting the first few days when instinctive shyness held them in check, the quadruplets rasped incessantly for succulent mice and young rats. I suppose matters could have been worse, but not much, for the hooked beaks were inclined to rip fingers as well as the sectioned mice.

Keeping Barn Owls successfully under captive conditions is, however, not as easy as may be imagined. They do not thrive on a diet of straight beef, mutton or horsemeat but must, for the sake of good health and contentment, be provided with the fresh whole carcasses of rats and mice, or hares and rabbits.

The hallmark of achievement, or should I say the ultimate seal of approval given by the birds themselves when conditions of housing and diet meet with unqualified approval, is a successful nesting event. Seldom, however, under restricted conditions have Australian birds of prey, let alone the nocturnal ones, scored such triumphs. We bred them first on at least four occasions back in 1935, in the special owl aviaries built in the centenary Australian section of Melbourne Zoo, and again half a dozen times at Healesville Sanctuary. Altogether we have records of over twenty-five

Opposite: *'Cinderella never performed such a fantastic metamorphosis before the ball as do these little Barn Owls from their earlier hideous days to the proud moment of first flight.'* Eldest bird (centre) is eight weeks old and ready for departure, with youngest owlet a week junior to it and still well clothed in down.

successful increases among those Barn Owls we have cared for, and there is intense satisfaction in knowing that the various progeny have flown off in a happy and vigorous condition.

Procedure then was standard in the case of the 1960 owlets taken from the Drive-In gum trees by Dudley McMillan, resulting in an early breeding event the following year. A male among these birds mated with a hen bird a couple of seasons his senior, and the first clutch of many following ones appeared.

Onset of a laying event was betrayed up to a week or more beforehand by the plaintive prolonged 'sk-airs!' of the hen bird. Always the nursery log appalled us—accustomed as we were to owls—by its insanitary condition, for invariably the birds discarded therein decayed and highly odorous bits and pieces. Amid this typical junk, often liberally whitewashed, Mother Owl carried out all incubatory duties unaided. She was quite insensitive to the general effluvia and also to the blow-fly larvae assisting to reduce the lower tiers of forgotten items. Needless to say the three, four, five, six or seven eggs were nest-stained in fairly short order. Brooding began on the laying of the first egg with an incubation time of thirty-four days for each. Thus, with some two days between each egg and perhaps a total of seven eggs all told, it means that among owlets there is a most extraordinary progression in size, with the oldest member up to a fortnight more advanced than the family baby. Quite often in periods of food scarcity the younger and weaker ones vanished—victims without a doubt of the insatiable appetites about them.

In steps and stairs then, because the eldest may be two weeks old while the baby is being hatched, these downy owlets are as incredibly ugly as their 'ghost bird' parents are beautiful.

Cinderella never performed such a fantastic metamorphosis before the ball as do these little Barn Owls from their early hideous days to the proud moment of first flight. As the down-covered 'ghosts' grow larger and more vigorous, feathers replace the soft thick down, which flies into one's eyes and nose in sneeze-producing clouds every time the vigorous wings are flapped. From 'ugly ducklings' with long miserable faces, the birds fast develop into shapely beautiful owls with typical heart-shaped faces. Anything they can 'force-swallow' in the way of fur, bones and flesh, is thoroughly digested and disgorged typically in the surprisingly large bundles of unwanted fur and bones.

I have never forgotten the feat performed by one owlet which swallowed the foot, leg and thigh section of an adult rabbit, all the bones of which were disgorged in due course as clean as the proverbial whistle.

As they grow towards the stage of nest desertion at eight weeks, the struggle proceeds to keep them all in food and I know only too well what it is to be Poppa owl, swooping upon every stray rat and mouse—day as well as night. It is, in fact, a very exacting responsibility. Father owl accepts these second-hand goods from me with somewhat grudging grace, preferring to sway from side to side, wings outstretched, feathers bristled and beak snapping with interjectory hissing, as he warns the intruder to keep clear of the nursery.

Most young birds of various species newly out of the nest are unmistakeable juveniles because of a give-away downiness, an immature type of plumage or different coloured eyes, beaks, toes etc. Not so, however, the ever complaining young with their night-long chorus of 'air-sh!' 'air-sh!' 'air-sh!' of these useful mouse-destroying Barn Owls.

In fact, when they desert the hollow at eight weeks and perch alongside their parents in some secluded spot, only an expert can tell the children from the parents, for it is a peculiar characteristic of Barn Owls that nest-leaving young are clad in grown-up dress. Only a slightly more profuse breast spotting and perhaps a very faint tinge of rufous about the neck, may be distinguishing features. Emphasizing the bewildering closeness in size and appearance of immature to mature Barn Owls is the precaution we are forced to take in ringing the legs of parent birds to be able to tell them apart.

One of them, shown hissing, swaying and snapping its beak as a bluff in a picture in this chapter, is typical of a species which has spread under its own steam over oceans and continents to most parts of the world, wherever rats and mice scamper for the taking.

The idea of banding younger birds with official numbers before giving them liberty in the great open spaces, is of course to learn, possibly, whether or not an early urge to travel takes them far afield before they settle down to some sort of localized life.

Chapter Ten

Goliaths among Masked Owls—
in Particular 'The World's
Largest Barn Owl'

In any account of the *Tytos* or Disc-faced Owls, it is as well to remember that recognized species additional to the Barn Owl are the fine Sooty Owl, the lanky Grass Owl and the Masked Owl proper, which, in Tasmania particularly, is the biggest and most powerful of them all.

Size notwithstanding, it is once again a matter of great difficulty to get to know the Masked Owl *(Tyto novaehollandiae)* or even to observe it casually, because it is a strict daytime recluse inside old hollow trees, caves and blowholes—particularly on the Nullarbor Plains. Hidden away it soliloquizes, drowses and disgorges the odd pellet until nightfall, secure from enemies and the harassing tactics of busy-body birds and nature observers alike.

Nevertheless, though really uncommon by comparison with the wandering Barn Owl, this king-sized version of it is found over Tasmania and most of Australia with the exception of arid areas, and it favours open woodland in addition to forested range country. The bird belongs also to southern New Guinea, the Tenimber Islands, Manus and Boeroe. To date Queensland Museum has received only four Masked Owls—the first being from Enoggera (Brisbane) in 1905 and the last from Beerburrum, south-eastern Queensland, in 1958.

Surfers Paradise, Queensland, is evidently a port of call for nocturnal creatures other than holidaying human beings, for not only was it the locale of an almost pure white Barn Owl (and incidentally an albino black snake) but the scene also on 18 August 1964 of a visit by one of these fine Masked Owls.

I never thought to go 'bird watching' at Surfers, but following a phone call from Bob De Courteney I found myself on that particular morning racing to see what he described as a huge owl perched in an open Norfolk Island pine on the ocean front.

'It's sitting quietly,' he told me over the phone, 'and its bulk is three or four times that of the Barn Owl with which I'm quite familiar. The breast colour is that of an old cement bag and there's no doubt it's one of the Masked fellows, and a whopper too!'

Unfortunately the unusual visitor stood out like a sore toe and our arrival was just a shade late to prevent stoning by the inevitable small boys. The owl took off and was last seen winging inland towards Chevron Hotel. Intensive search through every tree-shaded garden round about revealed nothing until several streets away a lady, unaware of events, reported a big owl blundering into a near-by tree before flying over the Nerang River. Sad to say there were no Mickies (Noisy Miners) about that day. Otherwise they would have pin-pointed our quarry promptly and noisily.

In all probability the Surfers bird, which impressed all who saw it by size and plumage, was an immature, fat and inexperienced female fresh away from a hollow in some large forest red gum in the hinterland (Ski Lodge Gardens vicinity).

Apparently it flew east until the barrier of the Pacific Ocean proved the insurmountable puzzle that brought about a stop-over that morning in an esplanade tree.

If we include Melville Island, five Australian races of the spectacular Masked Owl are recognized—largest of all, as mentioned, being the truly magnificent Tasmanian bird *(T. novaehollandiae castanops)*. Claimed by some authorities as a distinct species, it is regarded, however, by Mees (*Zool. Verh.* No. 65, 1964) as a race of the mainland Masked Owl run to size and darkness. There is no evidence that this bird ever migrates to the mainland, and supposed records for Victoria are probably due to lack of appreciation of the variations in the main continental race.

John Gould, that ornithological genius, who in the difficult 1830s to 1840s carried out such accurate pioneering work among Australian birds, was greatly impressed with the giant Tasmanian representative and recorded in his notes that it was a bird distinguished from all other members of its genus by its great size and powerful form, and that it held pride of place as 'the largest Barn

Owl in the world'. That is exactly what it is, and it is quite uncanny how this giant version of the common Barn Owl *(Tyto alba delicatula)* reproduces on a commensurate scale the general appearance, the antics, the nesting habits and similar varied calls to those of its smaller, and far less robust, relative.

Length measured from beak to tail tip really gives no idea of size in any member of the short-tailed Tytos, but it is no exaggeration to say that the female Tasmanian Masked Owl is quite close in stature and in the development of its toes and talons, to the Powerful Owl of the mainland. A glance at the accompanying picture of immature birds of both species sitting side by side gives some idea of this fact, whereas the measurement at maturity gives seventeen inches at the most for the Tasmanian Masked species, as compared with twenty-four inches in the case of the Powerful Owl.

So we have an island species capable of dealing readily with bandicoots, ring-tailed possums, rat kangaroos and the present-day rabbit. Doubtless, if necessary and not being above feeding on the ground, it could also manage pademelon wallabies and the quoll or native cat.

In Tasmania the big owl is quite notorious as a despoiler of rabbits caught in spring traps, and very often the head of a poor doomed bunny is eaten off on the ground at the site of its downfall. The size of pellets of bone and fur disgorged by female Tasmanian Masked Owls eight to ten hours after a feast is nothing short of phenomenal, for they may actually be larger than those cast by the Powerful Owl and compare favourably with the huge pellets thrown out by the giant Eagle Owl *(Bubo)* of Europe. The answer to the fact that these Tasmanian birds may produce cylindrical pellets three and a half inches long by one and three-quarter inches in diameter lies, of course, not only in the ferocious appetite of the birds but in the exceptionally wide gape of which owls of this long-beaked family are capable.

The great disparity in size and colour of plumage between the sexes of this southern Masked Owl is a truly remarkable state of affairs that in earlier days gave rise, understandably, to a good deal of confusion, particularly as the smaller Tasmanian male owl often bore a close resemblance to its namesake of the mainland.

In the case of the particular Tasmanian Masked Owl pair, the activities of which are the subject of review in these pages, the total weight of the male bird was found to be 1 lb. 5 oz. and his length fourteen and a half inches, against a corresponding weight

114

and measurement of 2 lb. 13½ oz. and seventeen inches respectively in the case of the female. Weighed in a sugar bag hung from a spring balance, the indignant birds objected most strongly, but we proved the fact that the hen bird is more than twice the weight of her mate and that, plus her more aggressive nature, is a combination to reckon with. Disturbance of either bird, in situations where ready flight is not feasible, brings about an inevitable joint reaction of a large output of odorous faeces and the striking of a bristling defensive attitude with the birds standing high on their long legs, wings spread wide and down, accompanied by slow rhythmic swaying from side to side, snapping beaks, hisses and an intensive glare from hostile eyes. Both birds are seen to advantage whilst employing these remarkable attitudes of bluff, and the contrasting hues in plumage are most marked.

On the upper surface the large female, who wore what is generally typical of well-dressed ladies of her kind in Tasmania, was strongly rufous-brown with primary and secondary flight feathers barred alternately rufous and grey-brown. The neck above is dark brown with the facial disc a deep chestnut-edged black. The lower surface, including thighs and legs, is generally rufous-brown with large and plentiful brownish dots on chest, abdomen and flanks.

On the other hand, the cock bird may be so much smaller and so different generally that it could pardonably be assumed that one was dealing with another species altogether. In this case the upper surface and wings were best described as yellowish brown, the facial disc white with chestnut tinge fringing the eyes themselves and the disc had the usual black edging. In contrast the underparts, abdomen, breast and legs, were whitish fawn with a light scattering of very small, pale brown spots, while round the lower neck a more marked tinge of fawn was noticeable.

According to Sharland (1958), a percentage of birds in the south and central parts of Tasmania are light-breasted, while in the north they are mostly cinnamon-tinged on such parts. Therefore my two birds could have come from widely-separated localities. Without doubt, over a range of individuals of this fine Tasmanian bird, there is considerable variation as to the hue of face, neck, under-surface and thighs. Gould noted that the under-surface of some birds was a deep rusty yellow, but in others the same parts were slightly washed with buff, whilst others again had the face a dark reddish buff approaching chestnut, and the under-surface much lighter. 'Whether the white or tawny plumage is characteristic of the adult,' he wrote, 'or whether it is influenced by season, are points that might be cleared up by residents of Tasmania.'

In view of the plumage variation between male and female, and in the light of experience gained in breeding these birds, I have been able to determine at least that there is no seasonal variation and in the case of both male and female offspring the young birds—once out of the down—have developed plumage of similar hue and pattern each in accord with its parent of like sex. Since that time, and over years as far as it is possible to determine, they have varied in no important particular whatever.

In the absence of records to the contrary, it appears that the Tasmanian Masked Owl was first bred in captivity by Miss Audrey Lee in a Launceston (Tasmania) collection in 1945.

Unfortunately, as far as I know, there is no written compilation of the activities of the birds at that time. My own experience of this exciting bird, though now quite a lengthy one as regards captive owls, is very limited concerning the species in the wild. The only occasion I met it, in fact, was in February 1946 on a very black night in a myrtle *(Nothofagus)* forest on the Franklin River below Mount Gell. There in this sombre, lonely, wet part of cold south-west Tasmania where we were trailing the marsupial wolf, a parent bird was feeding a wheezing, ever-complaining, fluffy owlet and in the darkness I did not dare to follow the pair too far into the tangled brush of horizontal scrub and numerous other obstructions, running for miles on each side of the disused tramway, once used in the transport of King William pine logs.

As far back as 1935 I had a female Tasmanian Masked Owl and a female mainland Masked Owl, housed together in an aviary where both birds laid clutches of eggs and sat side by side—naturally to no purpose.

However, in March 1946 during a trip to northern Tasmanian areas concerned with the establishment of koalas in a particular district, I met Mr F. R. Dowse of the Launceston City Park, and in return for aid with the native bears, I was able to select a true pair of Tasmanian Masked Owls from eight or nine of these fine birds in Mr Dowse's care.

Using four large living trees as uprights, we built a roomy secluded aviary for these 'treasures' in the outer area of Healesville Sanctuary, and there awaited developments.

Since that time it has struck me as more and more extraordinary that the eggs of this species, had, up until that time, been listed as

'Giant powder-puff': an idea of size in a young Tasmanian Masked Owl, 6½ weeks old, showing voluminous down on back, breast and crown.

Young Tasmanian Masked Owl in defensive pose, wings outspread, swaying from side to side and uttering prolonged 'churring' notes. The mask is developing and wing feathers growing—age 6½ weeks. Note massive covering of down.

Young Tasmanian Masked Owl (left) at approximately the same age as a Powerful Owlet. Though smaller, its voluminous fluff gives the impression of larger size than it actually possesses.

Tasmanian Masked Owl pair. The male (light bird) is less than half the weight of the female who also has far more powerful feet and bigger talons. There is a big difference in plumage and also in the hue of the facial masks. Both birds are on the defensive, swaying from side to side, beak-snapping and hissing. The female bird is crouched down to half her normal stature.

Male Tasmanian Masked Owl caught in the act of disgorging a pellet.

undescribed: for depending on food supply, it is very obvious, as in the case of the Barn Owl, that this giant species will nest and continue to nest irrespective of seasons. It and its related members are in no way seasonal, as all members of the genus *Ninox* appear to be. Conversely, of course, it is noticeable that Barn Owls breeding and thriving in the presence of abundant mice and rats go to pieces and die off in numbers should these animals become scarce in winter time. Possibly the abundance of small marsupials in Tasmania is a guarantee of livelihood for the larger Masked Owl and a vital factor which has contributed perhaps to its evolution.

In 1935 Mr A. J. Elliott described and illustrated the finding of two Masked Owl fledgelings within nights of one another outside a dry hollow nesting tree in cleared hill country at Cambewarra, New South Wales. In the *Emu*, Vol. 34, Part 3, he gives the date of the first discovery as 24 July, which would take the initial nesting activities back to early April. It is also significant that, though the nesting site was close to the home of this keen observer, only once in six months residence prior to July had he heard calls that could be attributed to them. An interesting point of contrast with the Hawk Owls *(Ninox)* lies in the fact that one and all of the Masked Owls appear to project most of their various whistles, trills, shrieks, screeches and squeals via a more or less open beak. There is no such thing as the closed beak double call characteristic of Powerful, Barking, Boobook and doubtless Rufous Owls.

On 21 August 1949, Merv Goddard who has no record of the Masked Owl in the Tenterfield area (haunt of both Sooty and Powerful Owls) climbed a giant flooded gum towering above a venerable Antarctic beech on a forested ridge of the Dorrigo tablelands, New South Wales. An adult Masked Owl *(T. novaehol-landiae)* flew out of a hollow eighty feet up, where investigation revealed a recently hatched owlet, one chipping egg, another egg still incubating and the leg of a rabbit.

In a similar discovery by Mr E. L. Hyem, the date was mid-July (1963), the height of the large hollow eighty-one feet, the tree also a flooded gum standing at the bush edge on a forested hillside above Pigna Barney River (Upper Manning district, New South Wales), and the egg number an exceptional four.

With the advent of July 1946, following three months' residence

Opposite: *Female mainland Masked Owl* (Tyto novaehollandiae novaehollandiae) *from south Gippsland, Victoria. This bird has found the introduced rabbit a helpful source of food.*

117

in the Healesville aviary, it became evident that the male Tasmanian Masked Owl had commenced a courting performance. As soon as dusk fell each evening, he began incessant chattering calls to the hen bird as he stood inside an elevated hollow log, alternating this vocal persuasion with a vigorous scraping using one foot after the other to form a depression in the rotten wood of the 'floor'. This twittering, ticking repetition of the same series of quavering shrill notes, each running shakily down the scale, was a performance that ran on and on each night, being a very near approach to the entreating cries of young Darters as they shake their ever-hungry mouths for food.

Courting activities carried on for several weeks, with both birds using the normal call note of the species a good deal as well. But for its greater volume, this cry is practically identical with that of the Barn Owl and mainland Masked Owl. It is a drawn out, rasping 'cush-cush-sh-sh' or 'quair-sh-sh-sh', according to the fancy of the listener. The cock bird usually redoubled his twittering on those occasions when his eloquence had been rewarded by the appearance of his burly partner on the porch of the log.

On 18 July the female abandoned her routine roosting spot on a secluded perch by day, though it appears that normally the large females prefer to hide away in hollows more than the males do. Having now retired to the nest hollow where she laid her first egg on 20 July, the female became a complete recluse, scarcely ever being seen outside day or night until nearly three weeks after the hatching date.

The second of the clutch of two eggs—dull white, elongated and slightly larger than a bantam egg—appeared on 22 July, forty-eight hours after its predecessor. The female now could not be frightened in any way and refused to budge from her nest. Whenever I mounted a ladder and peeped in she waxed increasingly indignant, swaying slowly from side to side with lowered head, snapping beak, ruffled feathers and spread wings, uttering the whole time a sustained rasping churring noise interjected with brief hissing. The male usually flew away and looked back from a perch, betraying anxiety by side to side head movements. His belligerent spouse, however, fitted by nature with superior size and strength, could, and would, fight an intruder to good effect.

From the laying of the first egg she brooded continuously *without relief at any time by the male,* though he was most diligent and efficient at all times in collecting and carrying food into the hollow.

Dead rats, pieces of rabbit and odd mice could always be found propped up in its various side crannies.

As previously recorded, no sign of the female outside the hollow was observed, though with the steady progression of the brooding period it seems obvious that she must have journeyed forth for an occasional drink. Members of the Barn Owl group, however, are not noted for nest hygiene and are entirely different from such species of *Ninox* as the Boobook, Barking and Powerful Owls. Their (the Barn Owls') home sites usually become increasingly offensive, for nothing seems to be carried away, and bathing, if indulged in, does not play the important part that it does in species of the Hawk Owls *(Ninox)*.

Following a lapse of three weeks the eggs of the brooding Masked Owl had become very definitely nest-stained with a patchy brownish appearance, and though glimpses of them could be obtained as the bird swayed from side to side, it was impossible to persuade her to come off; as she was ever ready to snatch violently with her talons, interference of any nature had to be exercised with great caution in order to avoid breaking the eggs.

The male normally perched close by the hollow in a dark corner but was occasionally to be seen by daylight just within the entrance of the nesting chamber. There, perched on one leg, with eyes almost closed and the lower part of the facial disc pinched in giving it an excessively heart-shaped appearance, he presented the typical sphinx-like appearance of this species in repose, which is markedly shrunken and statuesque in contrast with its alertness and bristling poses when awake and on the move.

On 23 August, just five weeks after the laying of the first egg, a single owlet was hatched—i.e. an incubation period of thirty-five days as compared with thirty-four in the case of Barn Owls I had observed previously. Now, even the cock bird with his new status of parent was inclined to a slight degree of belligerency, and for days after the great event he perched regularly by day inside the hollow, evidently stirred to his solemn depths by the shrill chirruping of the little owlet. The remaining egg was apparently infertile and failed to hatch.

By 4 September, at the age of thirteen days, the youngster's eyes had opened and gained sufficient vision for it to distinguish an intruder, so that from a partly hidden position beneath its mother's feathers, it would add a weak, rasping undertone to the general show of defiance. It was just as incredibly ugly as similarly-aged young Barn Owls, with disproportionately long bill and a 'miserable' undeveloped 'face'. However, fluffy down covered it thickly. Every item of food such as rabbits, rats, mice etc. was delivered express by the father bird, with the result that the interior of the hollow remained repulsively and consistently odorous.

On the night of 18 September, with the youngster almost four weeks old, the female was seen outside the hollow for one of the first occasions since the inception of the breeding period, but on my ascent of the ladder to the nest, she flew in quickly ahead of me and added to the owlet's clamour in beak snapping, prolonged churring defiance and grotesque swaying antics.

On 7 October when the chick was aged forty-six days (six and a half weeks), glimpses of the youngster had prompted me to take the law into my own hands and remove the truly magnificent owlet for the purpose of photographic records. It was no longer an 'ugly duckling' but a most attractive and beautiful young bird. We christened it, rather appropriately, 'Giant Powder Puff'. The facial disc with radiating feathers had developed sufficiently to alter the bird's expression completely and long, dense, woolly down stood out all over its body in profusion and confusion. That on the crown projected far enough upwards and forwards to shadow the face. Wing feathers progressing towards a stage of early flight, tail stubs and feathers of the mask were all that relieved the great ball of white down; seemingly this youngster, which proved later to be a male, was equivalent in general size to a young Powerful Owl of similar age.

In fact, several days later through a sheer stroke of timely fortune, I was able to secure a young Powerful Owl and persuade him to perch beside the Tasmanian juvenile for the fraction of time necessary to obtain the accompanying illustration. It is obvious that, downy and attractive as is the young Powerful Owl, it appears merely as a 'shorn sheep' beside the voluminous fluff and snowy whiteness of the immature Tasmanian Masked Owl. From this stage of maximum fluffiness, feathering gradually began to replace the down; at the age of two months (nine weeks), the young bird made its first nocturnal excursion away from the hollow and thereafter became increasingly venturesome. It uttered continuous complaining versions of the 'quair-sh-sh-sh' call of the adult, doubtless as a spur and reminder to its parents that its appetite was nowhere near appeased. By the time its age had reached three months the owlet was sufficiently developed, with the exception of down still

120

adhering to its flanks and thighs, to pass as a fresh and very hand-some edition of its father, and it began to look for its own food.

Examining the plumage of this bird in retrospect from this time, November 1946, it is safe to say that there was no variation in the hue of its feathering after the age of three months, with the exception of a slight intensification of the buff tinge about the lower neck.

At this stage, also, a retracing of steps is interesting in emphasizing how this large species of *Tyto* reacts similarly to its small Barn Owl relative under similar conditions of plentiful food and congenial environment. With the youngster still in its comparatively helpless stages and yet a close inmate of the nesting hollow, the mother did not await its departure but laid the first egg of a second clutch on 2 October. On this occasion she produced four eggs between that date and 8 October, and immediately began brooding with the laying of the first egg. However, the large owlet continually upset its mother to such an extent, by wing exercises and blundering playfulness, that eventually every egg was broken.

It seems very obvious that in the wild the parents would probably have chosen another hollow in the same general vicinity. Later in this month of October, transference of the adult birds to an entirely new enclosure provided with a suitable lofty hollow, soon found the cock bird in full courting performance again each night, repeating his twittering, ticking, rattling overture again and again. Both birds employed the prolonged rasping 'quair-sh-sh' referred to, at times, by some observers as a scream, though to my mind such call is by no means startling enough to justify that description and is therefore undeserving in the case of this species, and those of the Barn Owl and the mainland Masked Owl, of such an interpretation.

Call notes of the little-known Sooty Owl have recently revealed much of interest but though there are departures in several important particulars this bird can be recognized by voice alone as a derivative of the same general stock.

By mid-November 1946, the female Tasmanian Owl had laid yet a third clutch of eggs, this time numbering three. These were carefully removed and in the interests of a first examination and description, were forwarded to Mr Norman Favaloro of Mildura, Honorary Ornithologist to the National Museum of Victoria.

As already mentioned, to be truly successful with these nocturnal birds of prey, a tremendous amount of attention in the provision of fresh rats, mice and rabbits is necessary, and with other diurnal birds of prey to consider, it was difficult to allot this particular pair of owls more than a good health allowance of tucker. It was obvious that the suitable environment already present plus varied and plentiful items of food would have seen them nesting extensively. In the late summer (February/March) of 1947, in spite of interference to home duties by two extra birds of the species in the same enclosure, the parent birds set up house once more, and this time hatched and reared a strong female owlet, the plumage of which, on emerging from the downy juvenile stage, proved once again to be a facsimile of that on its mother's side.

Throughout the eleven months of 1948, though isolated from others of their kind the parent birds were housed, by force of circumstance, in a far from ideal aviary; here, though quite healthy and well, they reacted as expected and failed to make a success of various nesting ventures. Only two lots of eggs were laid, the first in mid-February and the second in early September, each clutch consisting of two eggs, but not one proved fertile. Then I was able to improve the housing conditions and in November 1948 with rabbits quite plentiful, and therefore readily secured, the male owl twittered regularly at night as he courted his mate towards yet another laying event.

Here then is the remarkable case of a large species of owl, hardy and evidently prolific, limited perhaps in mid-winter nesting on its island habitat owing to adverse effects on food supply, but showing here that it will breed irrespective of season, be it summer, winter, autumn or spring. How strongly it is at variance with the strictly seasonal members of the Hawk Owl, genus *Ninox*.

In view of the fact that the set of three eggs from these owls sent to Mildura were again a first from the species to be described, Mr Favaloro's report is of interest. It emphasized that they were oval in appearance, dull white in colour, with a shell texture fine and smooth tending towards a very slight gloss. Specimen A exhibited a small limey nodule towards the larger end. 'It is interesting to note,' he wrote, 'that these eggs differ considerably in shape from those of the *Ninox* group which are characterized by their spherical form, and although they have a closer resemblance to those of the Barn Owl they are so much larger, stouter and closer grained, that they could not possibly be confused with them.' Specimen A measured 47.8 by 35.0 mm., Specimen B, 47.5 by 36.0 mm., and Specimen C, 47.5 by 37.0 mm.

Chapter Eleven

Long Shanks Owl of Grass and Water Meadows

One or another of the Masked or Monkey-faced Owls is adapted for life in most types of the Australian environment and perhaps the rare Grass Owl *(T. longimembris),* though not confined to our continent, represents an extreme in specialization.

Much the size of the male mainland Masked Owl, he is the 'Daddy Long Legs' of the *Tytos*—fitted, like Swamp Harriers among hawks, with exceptionally long, almost bare legs all the better on the ground for a more comprehensive view and quick take-off against the menace of intruding predators, such as foxes, dingoes and quolls. Additionally, in the pursuit of prey in swamp and tussock growth, it is far more helpful for snatching successfully in downward drops among low vegetation to possess a good reach.

Associated with its life in open dwarf vegetation where obviously a Barn Owl's whitish plumage would invite quick attack by day-flying raiders, the Grass Owl is wonderfully camouflaged for survival. Consequently, in a paddock on the ground it is very much at one with its surroundings and, unless flushed from seat or squat, could readily be by-passed. Nevertheless, this far from conspicuous bird is rich in colouring—dressed above in dark brown admixed on wings with buff almost orange-yellow, whilst a bluish-grey wash is evident overall in flight. Underneath, breast and abdomen are tinged orange-buff with a scattering of brown spots.

Antics of swaying, beak-snapping and hissing are reminiscent of other *Tytos,* but the familiar facial mask is pinkish, spotted with brown. Coloured dark brown on its top edge like the rest of the upper surface, the disc is buff on the marginal cheek and chin sections so that in conjunction with its life in the open, the Grass Owl is much more of a two-tone bird than its tree dwelling cousins and would be highly difficult to distinguish whilst brooding eggs motionless underneath the arches of grass or sedge clumps.

I have had a Grass Owl primary wing feather from the Clarence River before me as a memory refresher in writing, and always that yellowish-orange, white margined, brown barred 'flight' is a reminder of the pleasing richness and harmonious colour blending characteristic of this ground frequenting hunter of the night.

This remarkable bird, in which the relative size of the sexes is not clear but which seemingly is a follower of the family rule of large females and smaller males, has been collected in Australia, though not Tasmania, on but few occasions, and then on or near the coastline. Apparently none of the few records is located more than a hundred miles inland. There are at least eighteen sites on which Grass Owls have been collected between Thursday Island and the comparatively bare plains of Werribee, separating the You Yangs and Port Phillip Bay in Victoria (1933). Another point of discovery is the Victoria River in the Northern Territory and there is an isolated (vagrant?) case from Cranbrook in the south-west of Western Australia.

These queer, colourful and very attractive *Tytos* are obviously great travellers, for they belong also to the southern half of Africa, South and East Asia and the whole Indo-Australian archipelago. In this chain, however, the distribution is very patchy and the bird is completely absent from a number of the islands.

Even though the Daddy Long Legs Owl has never been found in the Timor group, its path of immigration to Australia is indicated (Mayr, 1944) by its occurrence in China, Formosa, the Philippines and Celebes.

From Australia it has colonized eastern New Guinea, where a possible local race *(T. longimembris papuensis)* inhabits mountain grasslands between 5,000 and 6,000 feet above sea level.

Graeme George of the Territory of Papua and New Guinea Teaching Service received two owlets of this race (?) at his Wapenamanda station near Mount Hagen on 31 May 1967. Notoriously insensitive to animal feelings, the New Guineans who brought in the young birds returned the following day with a parent Grass

Opposite: *Photographed by Eric Zillmann at Hartley's Creek Fauna Reserve, these Australian Grass Owls* (Tyto longimembris longimembris) *show characteristic rich orange-yellow tints of plumage.*

Triangular mask or facial disc of the New Guinea Grass Owl (Tyto longimembris papuensis) indicates that Grass Owls which dwell in open, well lit habitats have smaller eyes than any other Tyto.

Natives brought this Grass Owl to Graeme George of the New Guinea Teaching Service at Wapenamanda. It is a sub-species of the mainland bird, apparently moderately common in mountain grasslands around 6000 feet. Photo Graeme George.

Owl, plucked of tail and vital flight feathers. It did not survive.

At the time of arrival the young birds weighed 10½ and 8½ oz. respectively and a fortnight later both were equally heavy at 15 oz. Their further development is being followed with great interest from afar, for most unfortunately a strict quarantine ban aimed at prevention of accidental importation of virulent West Irian strains of Newcastle disease blocked any possibility of obtaining these island owls.

In 1929, Hugh Innes of 'Walla', Gin Gin, enjoyed far greater contact than is usual with the Grass Owl on his father's Hereford stud of 'Barolin'. Near Bundaberg, Queensland, this property has some three miles frontage to the sea, whilst a great deal of it is open plain country with normally a very heavy body of grass.

In the first instance while on horseback, Mr Innes disturbed a Grass Owl from an area of blady grass growing in a swampy melon-hole area well away from timber. Dismounting and scouting the area he discovered squats, or hides, with pellets of varying ages scattered around. These were fairly big and contained bones and fur of mice, which were plentiful thereabouts, and also beetle wing cases.

At different times during the period 1929-1933, Mr Innes had five or six further meetings with Grass Owls, all within a few hundred yards of the original spot. When flushed in daytime they settled in long grass a hundred yards or so distant, usually with a Pied Butcher Bird or so in pursuit. Their flight appeared fairly slow, with the long legs very noticeable trailing behind. On several occasions on moonlight nights out in the open plain country, Hugh Innes saw Grass Owls sitting upon fence posts but unfortunately he never heard them call.

He had moved to 'Walla' on the Gin Gin side of Bundaberg when his brother reported the finding of a nest among tussocks on 'Barolin'. Cattle mustering had disturbed a Grass Owl brooding on four or five eggs. Unfortunately by the time Hugh Innes got there a week later, beasts had evidently trampled the nest, for only scattered shell fragments remained. There is no subsequent report of Grass Owls on 'Barolin' and since he discovered unmistakable *Tyto longimembris* feathers inside a couple of dens, Hugh Innes lists the fox as one of the local causes of disappearance.

Opposite: *A young Grass Owl* (Tyto longimembris papuensis) *reared by Graeme George at Wapenamanda, New Guinea.*

Rarely collected eggs of the Grass Owl, usually four in number according to early records (A. J. North) are more elongated than is the rule with most owls' eggs and may be described as thick ovals in form, white shelled and, with the exception of a few limey excrescences at the larger end, the texture is perfectly smooth and lustreless. The first clutch from which this description probably comes was discovered in the Herbert River district, Queensland, by a Mr J. A. Boyd over ninety years ago.

However, in March 1917 (the *Emu*, Vol. 17, Part I) F. L. Berney discovered a set of six eggs at Torilla, eighty miles north-east of Rockhampton. According to this informant, the eggs were laid on such fibre as was trodden down by the owls moving about under a clump of big coarse grass about four feet high, situated on a half acre of dry land surrounded by swamp and marsh. Under this grass the owls had trodden a labyrinth of winding passages or runs and at the end of one such hallway lay the six eggs. Both birds were at the nest and measurements in millimetres of the eggs at the time are repeated here as a matter of interest.

(A) 44 × 32 mm.
(B) 43 × 32 mm.
(C) 44 × 31 mm.   average $= 43\frac{1}{3} \times 32\frac{1}{6}$ mm.
(D) 43 × 33 mm.
(E) 42 × 32 mm.
(F) 44 × 33 mm.

The colour was pure white and slightly glossy with a texture finely pitted with limey, irregularly distributed nodules, while the shape is described as slightly ovate.

The comment of Merv Goddard on this variability of clutch size is obviously on the ball when he claims that, like the Barn Owl, these Daddy Long Legs birds of the grass lands probably lay more eggs when food is plentiful. With Barn Owls this is an absolute fact borne out time and again both in captivity and the wild.

Very recently, 1965-6, bulldozing activities in the vicinity of Cairns, north Queensland, dispossessed two apparently immature Grass Owls which were forwarded to Mr John Orrell of Cairns, identified by him and passed on to Garry Zillfleisch, who accommodated the rare creatures at his Hartley's Creek Sanctuary. By courtesy of all concerned, and Eric Zillmann in particular, because he took the pictures during a recent northern trip, these are the subjects illustrated in the Kodachromes accompanying the text.

Some very real contributions to knowledge of the Grass Owl,

still understandably a bird of mystery, are contained in field notes from Mervyn Goddard and from an analysis of pellets collected by him in the Clarence River vicinity. From this particular camping ground there was hope, for quite a time, that we would be able to make observations on a nesting event, but as in the case of many another promising situation in Natural History, our hopes were not fulfilled.

In late February 1963 at Sunnyside, seven miles north-west of Tenterfield, northern New South Wales, Mr Goddard flushed a solitary example of the Grass Owl from a bower formed amid a four-foot stand of sedge in shallow water. The location was actually a small swamp about 200 yards across. Altogether the bird rose in turn from five different parts of the swamp when approached. Apparently there was no other bird present and on each occasion the owl rocketed suddenly to expose the back tint of bluish-grey. It sailed along parallel to the ground for fifty yards or so, then dived downwards for cover with the suddenness of a dropping stone. It appeared to land heavily, in fact so abruptly, according to Mr Goddard, that he almost expected to hear the thump of impact. He reiterates that this meteoric landing is characteristic of all those he has disturbed. Subsequent visits to Sunnyside revealed no further sign of this owl or any other.

It was not until late September 1964 that tireless bird observer Goddard, prowling on this occasion at Woolli on the Clarence River, North Coast, New South Wales, put up another Grass Owl. The site was an extensive water-meadow where Mr Goddard happened to be searching for the Ground or Swamp Parrot (*Pezoporus wallicus*). The solitary owl rose abruptly about ten paces ahead of him, glided some sixty yards, then plummeted downwards into the vegetation. Once again the bluish-grey wash of the bird's back was obvious during flight.

Just a year later in the same locality in water-meadow vegetation there was a further exciting day for Merv Goddard when he disturbed, separately, from their bowers 300 yards apart, no less than two examples of the Grass Owl. The water-meadow vegetation here was about three feet in height, level and very extensive with all the appearance of a natural plain. Each owl rose suddenly about six to ten paces ahead of the searcher, glided some distance then banked and dropped like the proverbial stone into cover. Once again, states Mr Goddard, he fully expected some kind of landing crash or thump but there was absolutely no sound. Evidently those long legs are excellent shock absorbers. A subsequent thorough search, particularly in March of 1966, failed to flush any owls and, sad to say, swamp drainage and land development threaten to destroy this unique habitat.

Fortunately, from a well used squat here, Mervyn Goddard had the foresight to collect odd feathers and seven disgorged pellets of very recent date. He forwarded these to me for examination and they were passed in turn to my friend Mr Jack Woods, Director of Queensland Museum, for an expert inventory of contents.

The first pellet contained a single skull of the yellow footed marsupial mouse *(Antechinus flavipes)*, unidentified post-cranial (which means of course ribs, leg bones, etc.) matter and insect remains. The second pellet held a skull of the eastern swamp rat *(Rattus lutreolus)*, unidentified post-cranial matter and further insect remains. The third pellet was particularly interesting in contents which comprised a tooth row from the pretty sugar glider *(Petaurus breviceps)*, a complete skull of the pigmy marsupial mouse *(Antechinus maculatus)*, further unidentified post-cranial matter, insect remains and relics of at least four birds (including mandibles). The fourth pellet enclosed remains of no less than six birds (including mandibles) and a fair amount of unidentified post-cranial matter. The fifth and sixth pellets were parcels of post-cranial remains of birds and the final pellet (number seven) contained not only bird remains, but also a fair amount of insect residue.

Thus it becomes obvious that the Grass Owl is a hunter of fairly catholic taste, all being grist that comes to the mill. Above all, it is significant that its activities are by no means confined to areas where it 'camps', for sugar gliders and marsupial mice are scarcely inhabitants of water meadows.

Chapter Twelve

Dark Raider of the Deep Brushes — Concerning the Sooty Owl

In any account of the rigours and heartbreaks of years upon the trail of the Sooty Owl, one might pardonably be excused for paraphrasing Baroness Orczy's verse on her legendary Pimpernel:

'We seek him here
We seek him there
Those birdos seek him everywhere.
Is he in Heaven
Is he in hell
That damned elusive Sooty Owl.'

For one thing this large sombre-plumaged bird is not only rare but most restricted in range, only a dozen or so specimens of the nominate race *(Tyto tenebricosa tenebricosa)* having been collected from the coastal fringe ranging from Melbourne to Brisbane, and another half dozen of a definitely smaller northern race *(T. tenebricosa multipunctata)* being known from a more restricted area centring on Cairns. Strangely enough the Sooty Owl has been reported on Flinders Island though not from closely adjacent Tasmania.

So well indeed has this remarkable bird kept itself out of the public eye, that the Queensland Museum possesses but one example collected in 1892 in what is now Enoggera. On top of all this, it is specialized for life in the deepest, darkest and most secluded gullies of heavy forest and rain scrubs having in fact, for size, the largest eyes of any Masked Owl.

While recent evidence, gathered in the main from a captive bird, indicates that it not only favours daylight roosting within giant hollow trees but it possesses the shortest tail of any Masked Owl, thus facilitating this particular habit. After all no bird with a long tail is able to rest comfortably, particularly on a floor, unless this member is free of contact with the surroundings. By comparison with other Masked Owls the Sooty bird's face is broadly rounded rather than heart-shaped.

For many years whilst trailing the Powerful Owl in central Victorian and Gippsland ranges, I searched diligently, also, for traces of the Sooty Owl which shares the bigger fellow's environment. In 1927 as a first year University student I remember standing entranced before the huge glass display case in Melbourne's National Museum, where imaginatively mounted specimens of male and female, with widespread wings, showed so clearly the far larger size and terrific talons of the Sooty hen. But in the words of the song it was to be 'forty years on' before I secured a living specimen.

The late Frank Howe told me of observing parent birds and a single owlet in a sheltered gully at Olinda in the Dandenong Ranges, but it was not until my last days in Victoria snaring Lyrebirds for government-sponsored resettlement in Tasmania, that I met my very first birds of this species.

Walking softly through a cool cloister-like passageway between lofty tree ferns over the rich humus of a gully floor below Mount Donnabuang, I had a momentary glimpse in 'the dim religious light' of two Sooty Owls perched in frond stalks some fourteen feet above ground. Below them the leaf-covered earth was liberally splattered with traces of whitewash. In spite of several return visits, that was my first and last glimpse, in the south, of these mysterious dark owls so wonderfully specialized for life in the heaviest forest. 'Outside' roosting of the two, may have had its origin again in the shepherding of an inexperienced owlet.

The success of subsequent observations is entirely due to the initial prospecting, wide-awake interest and unselfish co-operation of Merv Goddard of Tenterfield, who knows the by-ways of the wild country of north-eastern New South Wales as perhaps no other ornithologist in the country.

In the autumn of 1964 Mr Goddard took us in turn, to two widely-separated localities where on isolated occasions he had both glimpsed and heard Sooty Owls briefly, but in neither area were the birds either visible or vocal. With anyone else but Merv Goddard it could have been a figment of the imagination, but my belief in the unassailable accuracy of all Goddard reports is unshakable.

Most large owls attaining adult status are very local in habit—therefore intermittent observations in the pin-pointed areas are definitely essential. An account from my diary of a subsequent mid-November expedition to the tumbled region concerned, where the granite country falls abruptly from the Tenterfield Ranges 1,000 feet to the lower eastern country carrying the hurrying headwaters of the Clarence River, is typical of many expeditions devoted to that fascinating and very special quest.

'It was perfectly still and the large moon shone brightly through the towering gums as, burdened only with sleeping bags, we made slow progress from one remote gully across ridges to another. Ted Ottaway, 'Dot' my midget dog, and I intended a vigil on a range side overlooking one of Mr Goddard's Sooty Owl localities, there to listen for the particular sounds that might assist in fixing dwelling trees. No one carried a watch so it was a timeless night in a timeless land, with Boobook Owls calling sing-song and dusky gliders volplaning with shriek and bubbling gurgle from one mighty eucalypt to another. So had their ancestors rejoiced in the cool night air long before the ravages of the white man began.

'It was easy to mark the long-tailed creatures as their glowing amber eyes reflected vividly down the spotlight shaft. The last sounds I remember hearing after tethering Dot to a small log between us and drifting off to sleep, 'anchored' in my hiphole, was a harsh argument between Frogmouths and the faint and far away 'woo-hoos' of a Powerful Owl.

'Hours later, possibly at one in the morning, under an abruptly overcast sky, a presence awoke me. Something moved stealthily beside us to bound precipitously down a gully as tiny Dot raced forth, barking excitedly, almost dragging her log over Ted Ottaway.

'The light beam illumined two vivid green eyes, attentive ears, and the shadowy form of a large dingo—splendid in his momentary stance of hesitant inquiry. But for the fact that Dot had been tethered, even now he might have been tearing her up in the shadows.

'Now a great flare lit the towering tree trunks and crashing thunder rolled around the mountains; rain fell in roaring torrents with a blasting wind, falling boughs and dropping temperature.

Soaked like a couple of shags, with Dot wedged dispiritedly between my feet, we began the ordeal of the longest, wettest night in years.

'To move was to get lost. Endlessly Nature's heavy artillery stayed in action but towards dawn it muttered and flickered into silence. Aeons later again as we began to see the tree trunks, the feathered folk in the lillypillies of the great gully below began their welcome to piccaninny daylight. Strong clear notes of the Lyrebird over-rode the crack of Whip Birds, liquid notes of Rufous Whistlers, and the insistent 'chap, chap' of Yellow Robins—psalmists of the dawn. Innumerable trills from Fantail Cuckoos and varied notes of a variety of honeyeaters blended in the swelling chorus until it reached a crescendo of melody, more magnificent and more moving than anything we had heard in years of wandering. Not a single sign or sound, however, from the Sooty Owls. It was another of those trips.

'To return to base took time, which, added to the endless night, seemed to presage an extremely late breakfast. Then Ted Ottaway unearthed his missing watch. We had certainly lost all track of the hours. It was just 5.20 a.m.'

As the seasons came and went and trip after trip proved fruitless, even the quest for the Holy Grail appeared simple by comparison. Here was a bird rendered difficult of location not only because of daytime hideaway habits, but largely because it appeared to have no fixed time of nesting. Often there were evenings when high winds or rain rendered observations completely useless. One particular night as Messrs Goddard, Ottaway and I sat silently on the gully side close to our dingo visitation point, there were brief and tantalizing moments when a shadow swooped to a bough twenty feet above us, peering with swivelling head as it subjected us to an intent and far from welcoming gaze. Territorially disturbed, this Sooty Owl had arrived in answer to Mr Goddard's down-scale whistle, a mimicry of its usual cry, and its eyes reflected ruby-like in the spotlight beams. Then it was gone, to reappear no more. In later times the characteristic eye shine was to prove particularly useful in pin-pointing the birds both here and in another area.

Merv Goddard frequently quoted the findings of Lindsay Hyem of 'Mernot', Curracabark Creek, who pioneered observations on several pairs of Sooty Owls he had found after laborious search. In this upper Manning River district of New South Wales, Mr Hyem, a contemporary bird observer whom I had known by his high

Swaying, hissing, beak-snapping and holding wings out, down and up, male Sooty Owl of the northern race endeavours to bluff the intruder.

Caspar, the male Sooty Owl from Atherton Tableland, spreads his short wings at extraordinary angles, snaps his beak and sways in efforts to bluff the intruder. Like the Barn Owl, the Sooty Owl occasionally expresses emotion by bending its head to a position almost between the feet, and slowly shaking it from side to side.

The huge eyes (largest in any Tyto), round mask, short wings and sturdy build of the Sooty Owl. Profusely spotted above, this male bird is of the northern race, multipunctata.

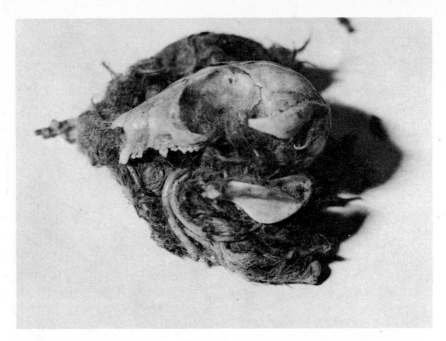

Unwrapped pellet found below Sooty Owl nesting tree discloses complete skull, ribs, small bones and fur of an unfortunate sugar glider. The disgorged pellet is 2½ inches long by 1½ inches wide.

Though clothed in dusky down, the baby Sooty Owl shown here is ready for flight. It is a member of the northern sub-species, multipunctata. Sooty Owlets are much darker at the nest desertion stage than they are in adult plumage.

Habitat of southern Sooty Owls in Warburton Ranges, Victoria. The author met a pair in this area in the late forties while snaring Lyrebirds for resettlement in Tasmania.

Depths of lillypilly Sooty Owl gully, rich in flooded (rose) gums and epiphytes. Here we sat at night listening for calls that eventually betrayed the whereabouts of the elusive birds.

Vine-tangled lillypilly and flooded gum gully in the Tenterfield-Grafton forest ranges,
N.S.W. Merv Goddard at base of the Sooty Owl nesting tree found after years of
search and to which it was necessary to cut a track.

Merv Goddard climbing mighty flooded (rose) gum (Eucalyptus grandis) on nylon ladder, to nest hollow of Sooty Owl. Forest country between Tenterfield and Grafton, N.S.W., 5 March 1967.

Lofty top of flooded gum in which Sooty Owls nested on the far side. These birds are the only Australian owls indulging in a courtship 'song' of pleasant twittering.

Flooded gum top towers above gully growth but is protected between range walls. Entrance to Sooty Owl nursery, 102 feet above ground, faces camera, with floor covered in old bones vertically down five feet to bulge. Photo Merv Goddard.

Female Sooty Owl 102 feet above ground in rose gum level with her nesting hollow, and fifteen feet from Merv Goddard who took the picture while clinging to his nylon ladder. She resents the intrusion.

standing most of my life, had found Sooty Owls with eggs and later with young, and informed Merv Goddard that he had only known one egg to a clutch except on a solitary occasion when there were two. He had also tutored Merv Goddard in the peculiar whistling scream, which at times (prior to egg laying?) is liable to bring either male or female rampaging along to repel invaders of his or her kind. For unlike the related Barn Owl, here is a specialized *Tyto* with a 'no trespass' sign out for others of its species.

In spite of the number of evening visits paid by Merv Goddard to the Clarence water-shed, interspersed less frequently by special trips of our own with or without our guide, philosopher and friend, the Sooty Owls in that gully actually nested and reared a youngster unknown to any of us. When you consider the primeval nature of the dense forest there with giant trees which had never seen saw nor axe, this was not really surprising. Suffice to say that on 16 September 1965, a crestfallen but very interested group of 'owl experts' watched a fine mobile young bird flying about after dark uttering incessant complaining calls—very like those of other Masked Owls—for hand-outs from invisible parents. That meant that the original nesting operations pre-dated this time by at least four months—the period probably being June of that year.

Now a remarkable interlude, or should I say, anticlimax, supervened. Eric Zillmann of Gin Gin, on tour of north Queensland, wrote in December 1966 informing me that Stan Stirling, whom I had met but once since earlier Melbourne days, was actually exhibiting a Sooty Owl in one of his Stratford (Cairns district) Fauna Reserve aviaries. It had been brought in three years previously, as an owlet, following rescue from a hollow tree felled on the Atherton Tablelands. Ridiculous as it may seem, following those years of wandering in rough places and so much intensive search, 'Caspar', a male representative of the smaller northern race (*T. tenebricosa multipunctata*), was delivered to me with the good wishes of kindly Stan Stirling per the standard services of T.A.A. and Greyhound Bus Lines.

Extremely attractive in his silver wyandotte type of plumage, and heavily spotted above in contrast to the southern race, Caspar was sturdily built with the unusually round face notable for a rufous corona radiating from very dark eyes. Our distinguished newcomer settled quickly and dined heartily on fresh rats and mice. In no time at all a number of unusual features came to light—the outstanding one being his undoubted rowdyism, and his sawn-off, almost tail-less, appearance. He found his voice within two nights of arrival and it was every bit as remarkable as his appearance.

On numerous occasions after dark he uttered, and still utters, the rounded downscale call which is neither scream nor whistle but in between the two. It proved to be, as we now well know, the usual deliberate Sooty Owl signal call that can be likened best to the sound of a falling bomb, without, of course, I am thankful to say, an end explosion, and by comparison with the mellower call of southern Sooty Owls, thinner and more penetrating.

Should Caspar be imitated, he works himself into a fury, snapping his beak repeatedly and uttering short ultrasonic screeches, one upon the other, which sound, for all the world, resembles that of a possum's claws scrabbling again and again for a grip upon new galvanized iron. At such times he is by no means above outright attack upon what he probably suspects is an intruding male of his kind. All this seemed quite remarkable for a bird so hard to locate and normally so very silent. Witness the swooping upon us by the male bird when imitations of the whistling call were made in Tenterfield gullies. Here we have parallelism with the Powerful Owl of the Hawk Owl group, in that intrusion upon occupied territory by others of the same species is not tolerated, whereas, interestingly, as in the Tenterfield localities, a Sooty Owl gully is also tenanted by a Powerful Owl pair.

Most surprising but completely reliable in this respect are the records of Mr E. L. Hyem indicating peaceful coexistence in the same area (upper Manning River) of forest and brush of both Sooty and Masked Owls (*T. novaehollandiae*)—this despite their somewhat similar diet and habits. Very remarkable indeed on top of this is the almost total absence of Powerful Owls thereabouts.

The long and the short of things in general, was that I purchased a tape recorder especially to be in a position to obtain a faithful reproduction of every kind of sound of which Caspar was capable. By this means we fondly hoped for spectacular reactions when playbacks were eventually made on the sacred home grounds of other Sooty Owls. Within a month we had several reels of such a variety of whistles, screeches and insect-like twitterings, that it became more and more obvious the Sooty Owl is not only a most specialized *Tyto* but, vocally, though recognizable as a Masked Owl, it differs considerably from its more stereotyped cousins. At all events on the night of 1 June 1966, remote from the madding crowd, Merv Goddard and I sat on a log in the depths of the same old mountain gully trying these recorded sounds on the local boys in feather and fur. It was a calculated experiment, knowing as we did that our will o' the wisp Sooty Owl and also a Powerful Owl definitely haunted the area. I had the voices of both species on this tape and the reactions of the territory-conscious night raiders were eagerly awaited. At dusk, the leisurely 'woo-hoo' of a resident Powerful Owl—always the epitome of that vast solitude—rose a few times from the gully head.

By the marvel of magnetic tape, a voice of his kind followed suit, daring to answer in the very heart of a forbidden kingdom. Soon and surprisingly close, came the challenge in the slow, deep voice of the male 'Eagle Owl'—somewhat of an individualist in that his call could be interpreted as 'ooer-hoo!' So bent on eradication of the unseen interloper was this fellow that he flew over our heads and perched above—perfectly spotlighted with winding head and glowing orange eyes. But this big owl was no fool, and deciding that a searchlight and reticent members of his kind could scarcely mix, floated off to call in the chilly distance. Perhaps something of the 'licorice allsorts' touch about my tape, containing as it did, owl 'language', the lights of Vienna, a Lyrebird concert, dingoes howling and the Hawaiian 'Lovely Hula Hands', also disillusioned him, for in the darkness the tracks occasionally over-ran. Suddenly from behind us came a rustle and scratch of nails on wood. Two blazing eyes reflected the light beam and there, perched on another log, evidently sure that these peculiar noises meant easy pickings, sat a beautiful fox. His I.Q. must have been lower than usual for he could have been a sitting duck and his eventual retirement was reluctant.

Time and again the weird whistle of the Sooty Owl plus the high-pitched chattering that goes with conversation and courting were broadcast. Then we heard it—half-hearted but definite—a mellow whistling reply followed by a series of chirruping noises. A Sooty Owl was there but in an off-season period could not be bothered coming too close, let alone repelling invaders. That was certainly a most interesting and highly diverting evening. One very certain thing was the continued presence of resident Sooty Owls in the lillypilly gully, but which of those hundreds of towering-barrelled, eucalypt colossi hid the upper storey flat, or flats, in which the pair resided? Further spring and summer trips were fruitless though a visit to another location, twenty-five miles along the Casino road, on a fantastically clear moonlight night, was notable for hours of chit-chat by a different Sooty Owl also replying to Caspar's message on tape.

Sunday, 5 February 1967, dated the major breakthrough on a day that I underlined in my diary as seldom previously. Alone in the night bush crawling through the thickest of gully jungle and beamed on excited Sooty Owl conversation, Merv Goddard actually saw one of the birds fly into a lofty hollow and remain there. An enthralling telephone message had its effect. 19 February found me encamped in the vicinity, firstly with Mr Goddard, and then for several days on my Pat Malone of all times in the terrific downpour accompanying the passage of cyclone 'Barbara'.

However, though the solitary confinement at this cool 3,000 feet elevation in dripping bushland was not particularly enjoyable then, in retrospect the impressions and new knowledge gained were unforgettable and most valuable. That dense tangled gully untouched by man, much as it existed in the days before Captain Cook, always overpowered one with its timeless immensity. Its creek of lillypillys or 'scrub cherries' (*Eugenia australis* and *E. smithii*)—thick and impenetrable—sheltered the massive butts of those enormous rose or flooded gums, towering high to spread colossal crowns of vast whispering foliage. The sweet 'why-yew', 'witch-you' of Black-faced Flycatchers, the chortling of Crimson Lowries, the ringing cracks of Whipbirds, thin calls of King Parrots, voices of Bower-birds, Fantails, Scrub Wrens, Cuckoos and many others, were music of a kind that never palled. Only the Lyrebirds (sub-species *edwardi*), not yet over the moult, were silent. Even now I recall the occasional roaring of wind high up on the range tops, the reedy 'tree-frog' call of Glossy Black Cockatoos, and then in a tranquil pause, the sudden grinding crack, rending tear and final roaring ruin as the whole gully jumped to the whooming crash of a tall eucalypt collapsing from a weakness accentuated by the extra weight of rain—I had been under it minutes previously. The birds paused only momentarily.

With the approach of night as I sat under Merv Goddard's discovery tree, Currawongs flew high calling in transit, distant Kookaburras farewelled the day and the awakening 'woo-hoos' of our old acquaintance, the Powerful Owl, were heard as he stretched a leg and wing on a hidden perch, prior to sailing abroad in search of some hapless possum-glider. Then abruptly the highlight of all in the almost complete obscurity of departed day began at a quarter to seven with a short mellow whistle of lost soul quality—prelude to the overhead courting performance of the Sooty Owls. Obviously they were preparing to set up house. One called from the top of a brush box and the other 110 feet up on the edge of a hollow in the gigantic rose gum. There was no repetition of the mellow downscale 'whistle', but again and again they conversed in duet and part duet in a series of down-rolling chirruping trills, for all the world resembling cricket sounds in pitch and consistency.

For the first time I was aware of a distinct difference between the calls of male and female. Of this there was no mistake because the big female sat at the hollow entrance where she performed with scarcely a gap in her continuous rippling session, while the Sooty male chirruped from the neighbouring brush box—my position being between and immediately below them both.

It was a fascinating and quite un-owl like exhibition of courtship —the hen bird's down-rolling chirrup unmistakably louder, running further downscale and being more rounded, as it were, in performance. With the birds calling either in turn or together, the delightful rippling conversation ran on and on—attractive and rather sweet in tone, with both owls still 'talking' half an hour later when I walked away into the blackness.

The tape machine had been running on an extra long reel since before dusk, so that beginning with cricket and Whipbird voices, the mighty roar of the falling gum, the gully birds saluting the dying day, the Powerful Owl welcoming the coming night and finishing with the fantastic duet of the Sooty Owls, it is certainly a unique and fascinating record.

Merv had picked up several pellets on the ground beneath the home tree, one of which measured nearly two and a half inches in length. On investigation I found it to be a neatly bundled parcel of sugar glider remnants. The ribs, broken leg bones, fractured remnants of pectoral and pelvic girdles and the entire clean unbroken skull (lower jaw included) were wrapped in the victim's fur. Surely these colossal ejections had been performed by the bigger female Sooty, for to tear off the glider's head and swallow it holus-bolus in the first place would call for an enormous gape and a most hearty appetite. Remnants in a second pellet were those of two sugar gliders (Queensland Museum analysis) so altogether, from large to small, the parachuting marsupials of that great gully would need to keep on their toes.

Many a drama must be enacted amid the dark world of tall rustling tree tops, under the stars, and little wonder that only the fit and active furry ones survive. There is no room for weaklings here.

As soon as he could take another daylight journey, Merv Goddard travelled up-gully again, securing his nylon ladder on the rose gum and scaling that mighty towering trunk into the world of leaves. The entrance hole to the roomy, musky-smelling owl hollow was situated 102 feet above ground, with insufficient room for Mr Goddard to poke his head in far enough to scan the whole floor six feet vertically down within. However, by means of a flashlight, he could see two fresh tails of ring-tailed possums, two apparent sugar glider tails and one from what would have been a half-grown dusky glider.

Remains of these recent victims with which the owls must originally have practically fallen to the nest bottom, were super-imposed on a mass of older bones of the various tree marsupials mixed among rotten wood debris of the floor. Obviously it was a robbers' roost of many years' standing. Apparently the hen owl scaled the wall and left the hollow before Merv Goddard reached the exit hole, for he says he was startled, on turning from inside observations, to perceive her—'a very large bird almost as big as a Powerful Owl'—level with his position and quietly observing him from only fifteen feet away.

It says something for his calmness of nerve and attention to detail that, precariously perched as he was, above his ladder, like a fly outside a tenth storey window, he turned about far enough to focus his camera and take the picture you see of Mrs Sooty looking back at him over her shoulder. Almost immediately, then, she dropped downwards, swiftly and gracefully volplaning round the trunk of the nesting tree, through a vine-covered brush box, to disappear completely, apparently into a hollow in a flooded gum some forty yards from the perch she vacated.

'Little' Mr Sooty was nowhere in sight, although almost certainly occupying a 'flat' in the immediate vicinity.

In view of the female bird's static behaviour and the lively courting activity that had entranced us over a period of weeks Merv Goddard reclimbed the 'depot' tree on 25 April (1967), sure that important events pended. It was a momentous date in more ways than one and almost his last day on earth, trees or anywhere else. Once again as he approached the top flat doorway, the hen scrambled up inside and flew out to perch in almost the same position as on the previous occasion. Prepared on this climb for just such a possibility, Merv took five pictures and just as he tried to get closer the sturdy owl flew thirty yards to a giant tallow-wood where she excreted, flying another forty yards to a branchlet of a flooded gum with a large rotted-out hollow section.

Into this she literally hurled herself two or three feet down—'plonk' into a hollow. 'This,' wrote Mr Goddard later, 'bears your theory out perfectly. The Sooty Owl is a short-tailed bird of the hollows—apparently it hates being outside for any length of time by day and I reckon this was the self-same hollow she sought last time, as her scream came from that very spot right on dusk.'

What a pleasant surprise now awaited the climber when he turned his flashlight and a home-made periscope into the home hollow. At the bottom of that 'mausoleum' of bones, fur and time-rotted wood, lay two eggs—the first he had ever seen. Here was a rarity in the southern race of Sooty Owl—a two egg clutch rather than the one and only which is usual.

Beyond the 'safety' of his nylon ladder and absorbed in the interest of what he was observing, Merv Goddard decided for the sake of records that he would strap his camera to an upright branch and take pre-set exposures of himself examining the nest hollow with periscope and torch. He manoeuvred his camera into position and while doing so stood upon a horizontal four feet long, four inches thick dead limb, upon which he had tested his weight on the prior climb.

He was adjusting the lens aperture—his position 102 feet up that mighty gum—when the limb under his feet fell soundlessly away, eventually hitting the ground far below with a sickening thump.

'I still can't think how I saved myself,' he wrote later, 'I think I held on with one hand to the fork some two feet above my head where the camera was tied. My reflexes must be excellent after all! I had no heart-beating aftermath. There was no time to realize anything. The event beat even fear reflexes.'

That from my colleague—ever a master of understatement—brings home the shave with death that climaxed a grand discovery. Looking at the machete-sliced 'stakes' of acacias and saplings shorn off for our 'track' about the great tree, Merv's imagination painted a grim picture for him on his return to earth. What with the gum that fell across the gully where I had been standing so long and now a near tragedy at the nesting tree itself, it seemed truly that the secrets of the elusive Sooty Owl had their guardians.

Merv Goddard delayed his departure until dark that famous day and saw the female return and enter the nesting hollow at 5.40 p.m. Seven minutes later, again, the much smaller male arrived on the scene and chittered trivially from a tree near by. At 6 o'clock the female reappeared at the entrance and the pair conversed in the twitterings that are so much a feature of their vocal performances. At 6.40 p.m. there were some harsher cries and the male flew off, presumably to carry out a raid for 'breakfast'. Merv Goddard started down creek on this lovely moonlight night at 7 p.m.

His most recent letter (about an experience on 19 May 1967) described contact with a 'new' pair of Sooties on Tea Tree Creek in the Tenterfield district, when not only one, but two birds, responded to his imitations of the whistle or scream.

The eerie sounds, deeper, as mentioned, than those of the northern Sooty, reminded him at a distance of a series of short howls and came from a side gully at 5.40 in the evening. Soon a twittering arose and making his way as quietly as possible towards its source, Merv got close enough to discover two Sooty Owls considering him—obviously also resenting his imitations of the 'falling bomb' whistle.

Continued intermittent whistles on the part of the intruder evidently increased the annoyance of one bird in particular, because it descended suddenly to a lower bough towards him with a heavy jolt, wings spread wide and downwards—meantime swaying menacingly from side to side. It came lower still with yet another solid limb-shaking jolt, obviously intimidatory, being now a mere thirty feet from the observer whose flashlight, by great misfortune, had weakened to the point of uselessness.

So Mr Goddard, who could not discern a difference in size between the indignant performer and the other bird sitting quietly near by, could only guess that the belligerent one was the male owl. Harking back to experiences with other Masked Owls, this indeed could most likely have been the case.

With completion of these chapters on the Masked Owls in general, the following measurements of eggs in millimetres of random clutches of the four species (after E. L. Hyem, M. T. Goddard and F. L. Berney) are of interest:

Barn Owl *(Tyto alba delicatula)*

	(39.5 × 32 mm.
one clutch	(41 × 33
	(42 × 33

Grass Owl *(Tyto longimembris longimembris)*
        (44 × 32
        (43 × 32
        (44 × 31
        (43 × 33
        (42 × 32
        (44 × 33

Masked Owl *(Tyto novaehollandiae novaehollandiae)*
        (44   × 35.5   (48   × 36.5   (45 × 34.5
        (44.5 × 35   (45   × 36   (43 × 35
                        (44.5 × 36.5

Tasmanian Masked Owl *(Tyto novaehollandiae castanops)*
        47.8 × 35.0
        47.5 × 36.0
        47.5 × 37.0

Sooty Owl *(Tyto tenebricosa tenebricosa)*
        (46 × 38   49 × 40   Single Egg
        (44 × 36.5   48 × 37.5 Single Egg
        (51 × 40   52 × 40.5 Single Egg
        (48 × 39

There is a graduation from the Barn Owl upwards, with the largest *Tyto* eggs of all on the mainland being produced by Sooty Owls. Surprisingly, they also exceed measurements made by Norman Favaloro of individuals of the clutch of Tasmanian Masked Owl *(T. novaehollandiae castanops)* laid in our Healesville reserve in 1946.

Since the foregoing was published much enlightenment has been shed on our knowledge of the Southern Sooty Owl (T. tenebricosa tenebricosa) thanks to successful breeding, no less than eight successive times, of a pair obtained as fledgelings by Mr Goddard at Boonoo Boonoo on 27 May 1968. They were reared and bred by me at West Burleigh, Q.

To summarize: A clutch consists initially of two eggs though usually there is but one survivor. Laying interval is four days. The Incubation period is lengthy—six weeks, with eggs appearances recorded for January, March, May, October, November and December.

Owlets remain in the nest for three months but are sufficiently mature for breeding in the brief period of thirteen months.

In view of the great discrepancies in size plumage and voice, I am now firmly convinced that further work will prove the designated Northern and Southern Sooty Owls to be two distinct species.

Rather reluctantly, in a two year period, a female southern bird successfully mated with a northern male. Two owlets of this union have developed successfully.

Chapter Thirteen

Owl-like Birds That Are Not Owls at All

1. The grotesque old Frogmouth

Probably the most frequent victim on Queensland roads by night is the large grey bird mistakenly known to the casual observer and most country dwellers as the Mopoke or Frogmouth 'owl'.

It is quite an excusable error since the great big eyes, noiseless flight and nocturnal habit fit readily into the owl category, but if those motorists who step out to see if they can do anything for the poor, old, broken-winged fellow sitting on the road or jammed in the radiator grill, only inspected his feet and beak, they would realize that these are not owl features by a long chalk. Old Mother Nature, with her genius for fitting specialists into every environment where they will make or break themselves, has a totally unrelated group of night birds vying with the smaller owls in collecting night-moving insects for a living and, like owls, shunning the daylight.

These 'false owls', typified by Frogmouths and the Owlet Nightjar, belong to a completely different order of birds (Coraciiformes) which includes families such as the kookaburra and other kingfishers, the Roller or Dollar-bird, the gaudy Bee-Eaters, the Swifts and Nightjars proper. Here apart from other features, you will get an idea of their true relationships in the general widemouthed, weak-footed, insect-chasing propensities of all.

Not a single member of the Frogmouth and Nightjar families is equipped with the narrow, strongly-hooked tearing beak and the powerful talon-shod grasping toes that in owls work so essentially as components of one another. In fact, to be facetious, if there is any

142

doubt, merely pick up the bird in dispute. Should it drive clutching, penetrating claws into your skin continually exerting cruel pressure, then it is definitely an 'owl' and *not* a Nightjar!

The Tawny Frogmouth even gained its generic name *Podargus*, in the first instance, from its 'gouty' feeble feet. Cuvier, a famous French naturalist, spotted this feature in the early years of last century and considered it of sufficient significance to provide a generic label.

Frogmouths stand out conspicuously from all other Nightjars (using that word in its most inclusive sense) because of their somewhat massive build, their ugliness, and the huge size of their beaks—the appearance and wide gape of which is the derivation of the popular name of Frogmouth.

The bird passes its life completely in the open, asleep by day in trees of forest, swamp or sparsely treed plain—never taking advantage even for nesting, like so many spry owls, of the shelter afforded by hollow spouts and holes in the big old gum trees.

In fact, the Tawny Frogmouth *(Podargus strigoides)* commonly but very mistakenly called Mopoke or Morepork (see chapter on Boobook Owls) has a tremendously wide habitat and is quite numerous and well known over most parts of Australia and Tasmania. Each year at Burleigh Heads, Queensland, alone, we have an average of forty birds a year brought in with various injuries suffered on roads within a radius of fifty miles. This does not include the greater number killed outright.

No bird is more wonderfully adapted to its exposed perching life than the Frogmouth, for its colour scheme, from each small feather with its mid streak of black to the tawny brown, sometimes reddish, general effect, is in perfect harmony with the great gaunt branches and the dead wood of gnarled eucalypts, acacias and other native trees. The birds choose comfortable limbs that match them, from a perceptive natural instinct, and a couple of Frogmouths at limb junctions of ironbark eucalypts are fantastic in their skilful blending of form and colour. The tail is 'jagged' and above the wide beak a bunch of stiff spiny feathers juts upward and outward. As a rule when sleeping, Frogmouths—for usually a pair haunts the same tree—sit in forks not too far distant from one another.

On the appearance of danger or possible menace, the birds immediately assume the sphinx-still attitude that is the most wonderful and characteristic of all their habits. Elongating and stiffening their bodies, they draw their feathers closely in, while heads jut straight out or up into the air. There, while necessary, they remain motionless—resembling dead, grey, weather-beaten, broken-off branches. The stiff feathers above the beak give a realistic finishing touch to this marvellous fractured-bough attitude.

The birds also employ a danger signal which resembles the sound 'oo-oo!' 'oo-oo!' It is uttered very quickly and gutturally and if one bird perceives an overhead bird of prey, it acquaints its mate of the fact in such manner and they both freeze on the instant. By mimicking this sound I have caused Frogmouths in captivity—otherwise extremely tame—to stiffen immediately, but being tame they soon come to know they are being hoaxed. While photographing a pair of Frogmouths some years ago, a hawk actually appeared and the birds, having no junction of branch and trunk and no suitable thick bough to crouch along, simply sidled quickly together and watched the hawk in a semi-protective attitude from this position.

Frogmouths as a rule construct their nest—a very crude and crazy fabrication of sticks—across the fork of a horizontal bough. The future nursery is but a careless platform of collected sticks, pigeon-like in its insecurity, and here the usual two white eggs are laid. While brooding the female bird sits lengthwise along the bough as usual, and assumes her broken-branch attitude on the approach of possible danger. At such times she is even more difficult to see than her mate who perches somewhere in the same tree, or in another close handy. However, if the birds are watched closely, it will be seen that a narrow slit of yellow eye is regarding every movement, and as you move about the tree your every action is kept in view by surreptitious head movement. Should you climb the tree the birds fly away quickly, perch in another tree and resume their curious attitudes, but once the intruder is out of sight, the jutting position is discarded in favour of the far more comfortable ordinary stance.

In December and January, the loose feathers of moulting Frogmouths about a daylight perch indicate the birds' roosting place, and at such a time of the year I think it is possible to trace more of the birds than you are able to do at other periods.

The nesting efforts of two quaint Frogmouths in the Australian section of the Zoological Gardens, Melbourne, during my curatorship 1934-37 are of interest, for there appears to be no previous and no subsequent record of these birds breeding successfully under captive conditions. In 1926, late in the month of September, in my own collection at Ballarat, a pair of exceptionally tame Frogmouths gathered fine sticks and a few roots and manufactured a flimsy nest on a shelf in their enclosure. The female bird took to her crazy little structure immediately it was completed, but unfortunately she laid no eggs, though she continued to sit closely for nearly two months. I was able to observe many new calls of these birds during the period and it is surprising what a variety of notes they use. Both birds would spend some time at the nest after nightfall and the female was in the habit of uttering a running continuous call which is best likened to the sound of a distant motor-cycle. With head bent forward and body swaying from side to side, she would maintain this series of rapid running grunts, sometimes for as long as a quarter of an hour. The male bird occasionally answered in similar fashion, and his call was even more rapid. The ordinary conversation of the species, so often heard in the bush by night, was used commonly by the birds at this time. The cock Frogmouth usually 'spoke' from the far end of the enclosure and the quiet, deliberate but penetrating, 'oom-oom-oom-oom' was uttered perhaps nineteen times before it ceased as mysteriously as it had begun, and a short interval followed before the mysterious call swelled into being again. It is an extraordinary bird sound coming from nowhere and vanishing into nothing once more. Rare arguments accompanied by wide-open beak threat produced loud harsh 'swearing'.

When flying round the aviary at night they sometimes uttered a croaking growl and during daylight another sound, used as a means of communication, was a series of notes beginning loudly and rapidly and suddenly dying down again. This was quite distinct from the danger signal already mentioned.

In daytime, displeasure at disturbance was expressed occasionally in a series of guttural petulant grunts uttered with open mouth. Cats, possums, and other furred visitors in the vicinity of the nest built by the birds were treated with scant ceremony. With fiercely ruffled heads, great glaring eyes, extended wings, and vigorous hollow claps of their beaks, the birds would attack and intimidate unwelcome intruders, so driving them away.

This brief account of the bird nesting so long ago is given because of the observation of intimate ways, many not possible in the case of the more timid pair with which we were highly successful in another way in the Zoological Gardens in the mid-thirties.

On 5 September 1935, the female bird in a large aviary in our

Australian section of the Melbourne Zoo, was discovered perched lengthwise on a wooden beam near the ground. Her nest consisted of a small uprooted grass sod and a six-inch nail, and on this precarious support lay a single egg. Next day it rolled off, breaking on the ground below.

By 8 September the hen Frogmouth had made another flimsy nest, this time of grass and small twigs on the limb of a pepperina tree in the aviary. The site had previously been prepared for her by means of arranging a hollowed platform of bark on the bough. Two eggs were laid on successive days, but again bad luck dogged the bird, for on 23 September both were lying broken on the ground below the nest.

For the third time, the persevering Frogmouth laid a clutch of eggs and on 10 November two young birds were hatched. Several Nankeen Kestrels inhabiting the upper parts of the aviary were immediately removed in case they should develop a taste for the dainty little birds. However, bad luck persisted and when three days old, one baby Frogmouth fell to the ground; its fellow suffered a similar fate at the age of eight days.

Rather in despair of success after this extraordinary run of misfortune, I surrounded the nesting site with prominent ridges of bark, but was rather afraid that the structure would not be to the Frogmouth's liking. However, keen interest was revived on 30 November when the bird made her fourth attempt. She laid her first egg on this day and sat immediately; another egg appeared the following day. For exactly four weeks the bird continued to brood very closely and at no time was she relieved by her mate. On the twenty-eighth day the first young bird hatched, followed two days later by a second. The quaint 'chicks' were solemn, tender little mites, clothed in white down, and the mother bird, who had been rather pugnacious and reluctant about leaving the nest even when brooding on eggs, now became positively savage. On more than one occasion she flew at me and knocked my hat flying. Her varying expressions and glaring yellow eyes, together with the unpleasant hollow claps of her strong beak, were well calculated to scare intruders away from the nest.

Naturally the diet of the parent birds had been varied a great deal throughout the nesting season and now, with the advent of fledgelings, the block or feeding table was spread each evening with a most appetizing array of chopped mice and frogs, finely minced beef, mealworms, moths and a shallow tray of earthworms. Not content with this alone, the parent birds hunted through the aviary and several times dead spiders, which had missed the gaping mouths of the young birds, were discovered entangled in the down of their breasts.

One chick made little headway and it was missing from the nest a week after hatching. Apparently it had died and one of the parent birds disposed of it. The growth of the remaining fledgeling was slow but it grew up to be a very healthy bird. At the age of three weeks it was quite a handful—its small eyes were open and it took a drowsy interest in its surroundings. It could plainly be seen projecting from the nest beneath its mother. When the chick was one month old the mother bird was forced to perch on the side of the nest, and both she and the baby adopted 'broken-branch' attitudes when visitors with brightly coloured apparel came within the field of vision.

The young Frogmouth left the nest for the first time on 1 February 1936, thirty-six days or roughly five weeks from the time of hatching from the egg, and its devoted mother sat beside it on a horizontal limb. Some days later it perched back in the nest again, but its powers of flight were now strong and wherever it happened to choose a diurnal resting place, its mother would perch protectively beside it.

Late in February, however, the young Frogmouth had become much more independent and it perched alone by day. Gone were the mother's fierce glare and bristling resentment of intruders to her former nesting sanctuary and she simply froze, as of old, when approached, and roosted in her usual haunts in the upper part of the aviary. Interestingly enough, we were able to establish from this young bird that the species is mature and old enough to lay eggs of its own in the following season.

The beak of the Frogmouth is actually an exaggeration, to a fantastic degree, of the type of catching device developed by birds in its own order such as Swifts, Rollers and more normal Nightjars; for after all the Frogmouth is merely a king-sized Nightjar. In consequence, it is still a general belief in Australia that the big grotesque fellow is superbly adapted for the capture of night-flying insects. Yet as Dr D. L. Serventy emphasized in a brilliant and revealing paper published in the *Emu*, Vol. 36, Part 2 (1936), almost every record of an examination of stomach contents suggests that it does nothing of the kind, but obtains the great bulk of its food from the ground.

As far back as 1848 discerning John Gould wrote 'that the whole contour of the bird shows that it is not formed for extensive flight nor for the capture of its prey in the air—the wings being short and concave in comparison with those of true aerial Nightjars.'

Yet the fact remains that there can be little doubt that originally the big, wide and very strong beak (capable among other things of an agonizing pinch as a retaliatory measure) evolved as the chief weapon in hunting flying insects on the wing. Experience in feeding Frogmouths and watching the behaviour of resident dwellers in our sanctuary area has shown me that they fly down at night from observation posts to pick up *moving* Christmas beetles, frogs, worms, centipedes, field crickets, mantids, stick insects, huntsmen spiders and carnivorous crickets, plus a certain amount of dirt and debris. Mice, small rats and even dead sparrows are relished if dropped within their beaks. Should the item prove too large for ready disposal then it is methodically beaten to a pulp before being swallowed piecemeal. I have often watched half-grown tree rats *(Rattus rattus)* disposed of in this fashion.

An inherent Nightjar instinct deters the Frogmouth from tackling food items *that do not move* which is the reason that most specimens in captivity need to have rations—be they raw meat, mice or dead insects—placed right in their mouths. Not many of the birds learn to pick up such delicacies readily from a feeding block.

Ground feeding habits of the Frogmouth are also at the root of their high mortality rate these modern times on the roads at night. Many insects are attracted to lighted zones and fall struggling upon the roadways there. Others drop and move below road junction and street light illuminations while centipedes, spiders etc. are much easier to see as they cross the open ribbon of road from cover to cover. So the poor Frogmouth flies down to grab easy and attractive meals and, cumbersome as he is at all times, is too slow off the mark for the inexplicable twin headlights bearing down on him at sixty-plus m.p.h. Unfortunately he rarely survives to be warier next time.

Dom Serventy has suggested three hypotheses to account for the Frogmouth's abandonment of its ancestral habit of catching food in the air:

(1) that the genus *Podargus* (Frogmouths in general) was differentiated in a region where the constant supply of night-flying insects was insufficient to keep these non-migratory

birds in life and health, particularly in winter time (see winter mortality in Barn Owls page 105),

(2) that the ground feeding technique began as a consequence of 'post sitting' in connexion with feeding—similar in fact to the habits of the bearded lizard in daytime,

(3) that the great clapping beak may have become over-specialized for aerial feeding and therefore now is merely a serviceable, if clumsy, tool for capturing ground food.

Whatever the explanation and however aberrant Frogmouths may be, their mode of life is obviously a successful and accomplished fact.

Tough and tenacious of life, persistent and successful breeders and comparatively rapid in attaining maturity, they thrive in a variety of habitats over most of Australia (Queensland—south of Cardwell) and Tasmania, and you will have gathered that almost anything fresh and small that runs, wriggles, rustles or undulates is set upon and swallowed with strict impartiality.

Largest of all Frogmouths is the handsomely plumaged New Guinea fellow *(P. papuensis)* found over most forest and wooded savannah in the big northern island, from sea level up to an elevation of 6,000 feet. It is said to utter 'ooming' calls like its tawny cousin, and at times to indulge in a weird 'laugh'. This Frogmouth overflows into Australia, inhabiting Cape York and country as far south as Mount Spec, near Townsville (Queensland Museum record).

Then there is the smaller Marbled Frogmouth *(P. ocellatus)* conspicuously tufted above the nostrils and also largely New Guinean, but found as well on the eastern side of Cape York down to Cooktown. Frequenting thick scrubs, it is said to perch by day in masses of thick vines and other tangled vegetation.

According to Mr Jack Woods, Director of Queensland Museum, there is no material at all in that institution of the so-called Plumed Frogmouth *(P. plumiferus)* of Queensland's south-eastern corner and New South Wales' adjoining north-east, but Keith Hindwood describes a skin of a Plumed Frogmouth in the Australian Museum reference collection agreeing with this species. Collected in northern New South Wales, the size is slightly smaller than that of an average Tawny Frogmouth, with a general overall colour of warm reddish-brown. The under surface is marbled and mottled—not streaked and finely flecked as in the Tawny Frogmouth.

In Hindwood's opinion the Plumed Frogmouth could be confused in the field with the rufous phase of the Tawny Frogmouth. Actually this 'species' is now considered to be one and the same as the Marbled Frogmouth. The sixty-four dollar question, as to whether the Marbled Frogmouth ranges through other parts of eastern Queensland, remains an intriguing possibility coinciding with Hindwood's further opinion that *plumiferus* of border regions could occur up through eastern Queensland from north-eastern New South Wales, though decreasing in size as one goes north, so fitting in with smaller reddish birds in the Australian Museum labelled *plumiferus* from north Queensland.

A Frogmouth-like call that I tried to trace in the dead of night in thick scrub at Kin Kin (Gympie district, Queensland) has always worried me, for it was far from typical of the Tawny species.

2. Phantom Owlet Nightjar is not as sad as he sounds

The tiny eight and a half inch long cousin of the Frogmouths is likewise not an owl, but superficially so like one that the nocturnal midget, smallest of all our night birds and not even the size of a Noisy Miner, is named Owlet Nightjar *(Aegotheles cristatus)*. Equally often it is referred to as the Fairy or Moth 'Owl' and the call note occasionally heard from inside a tree in daytime is a weird sighing 'chirr–chirr'. Floating through the bush by night, this gentle unearthly cry has the quality of lament one would expect from a lost soul doomed to a hopeless and eternal quest for it knows not what.

There is every likelihood that various races of the Owlet Nightjar inhabit the variety of far-flung habitats within the continent, for it ranges all over wherever there is forest and open timber in Australia and Tasmania. Mayr's publication on New Guinea Birds (A.M.N.H., 1941) lists a large southern race of our Australian bird and no less than four other species with various sub-species in and about the northern island.

Back from boyhood days I have every reason to remember the sooty-coloured, soft-plumaged Owlet Nightjar, for in one of their nesting holes, barely reached by standing full stretch on a precarious limb, I explored one day only to have searching fingers bitten by an intruding family of sugar gliders. The ensuing crash to earth as the bough gave way, and my bewildered wandering in a daze, left me lost in the bush almost the whole of a blazing summer day.

Like the hulking Frogmouth, the Owlet Nightjar is equipped with bristles—in this case far more pronounced—projecting about and beyond the wide insect-scooping beak. Doubtless they are sensory in regard both to hunting activities and to the measurement of hollow limb dimensions when the little ghosts retire from sight for the day.

The resemblance in miniature to the Frogmouth, to whose family (Podargidae) it is closely related, does not extend to temperament, for the 'monkey-faced' Nightjar is just as alert and quick off the mark as the larger Frogmouth is slow and clumsy. Yet the agile little bird combines a certain amount of ground feeding with its aerial mode of raiding insects—proof being furnished by several workers, particularly Dr Serventy, who examined Owlet Nightjar stomach contents finding flightless weevils, worker ants, small grasshoppers, millipedes and beetle fragments.

Seldom, however, is this tiny and very smart flitting phantom a road-toll victim but in forwarding one for identification, Jim Schollick mentions that it was killed on a highway near his farm, 'Oakview', Gympie district, Queensland. Probably, being abroad at the same time as the owls proper, the Owlet Nightjar is legitimate prey for such larger nocturnal predators, but I know of no evidence to support such a theory. Nevertheless the Owlet Nightjar goes to greater lengths to maintain its numbers than the ground nesting Nightjars. The usual clutch of white eggs laid in a leaf-lined nest in a hollow tree or stump is as many as three or four. Maintenance of fresh green leaves under the eggs is quite a feature of incubation.

Let me tell you about a Queensland Owlet Nightjar whom we named 'Bright Eyes'. While bulldozing trees for a dam site at Kooroongarra, Mr R. J. Taylor spotted the departure of this character's mother from a hollow limb in a falling tree. This led to the discovery of the lone Bright Eyes baby, which Mr Taylor felt duty bound to rear. Thenceforth for four long months he became, perforce, a hunter of field crickets, which with beetles and moths the fluffy Bright Eyes devoured as fast as they could be procured. Constantly he churred for more.

Before going bush in the timbered country with plentiful hollow trees on our West Burleigh Fauna Sanctuary, the almost domesticated Bright Eyes spent several weeks at my place flitting about the house by night and even picking the odd beetle (placed there for him) off a wall or picture rail, in flight.

He 'talked' constantly, flitting noiselessly and rapidly after anything that looked palatable, while in the small hours he called in that sudden churring high note so suggestive of what one might expect from the 'disembodied soul' floating alone in space. A strong light-shunning instinct bade him return to good cover by dawn, and mostly he sought shelter in a horizontally fixed tin. In the narrow confines of this metal shelter he often scratched his plumage by day with such a rapidly whirring foot action, that it produced a most realistic alarm-clock effect.

Then some years ago, clearing operators on 'Ardrossan' between St George and Dirranbandi, Queensland, demolished a hollow tree which in turn revealed triplet baby Nightjars, much younger in development than the stage at which Bright Eyes was collected.

They were as comical in appearance as the Marx brothers in their heyday. Clothed in fuzzy down, greyish-white in hue these fledge-ling Owlet Nightjars regarded all and sundry with great, forwardly directed eyes, for all the world like a trio of Marmoset monkeys. All their activities provoked mirth and rearing them for eventual liberation proved great fun. Should they shuffle backwards from an imagined danger it was done at the double, and likewise in seizing beetles, grubs and meat from one's fingers, they grabbed and swallowed in lightning gulps almost too fast to follow. So small were the individuals of this 'Snap Dragon' family of three, that all of them could sit comfortably in a single upturned hand at one time.

Though we hated to see these lively little fellows go bush their eventual departure brought sighs of relief, for the collection of grasshoppers, grubs and a thousand and one insects over the weeks was exacting indeed. Occasionally nowadays we flush Owlet Nightjars by scraping local hollow trees 'goanna fashion', but if one of these little ghosts is Bright Eyes or a Terrible Triplet, he or she is determined to keep the fact forever secret. Not only have they all returned to the wild but instinct of the ages has obliterated any education we may have provided.

3. The ground roosting Nightjars are past masters of camouflage

'On safari' in late November 1964 through dry ranges of the Burleigh hinterland, Queensland, to reach gully pools where he collects our platypus food crustaceans, Alec Wilson returned with tales of a 'Night Hawk' that uncovered a fluffy chick as it flew reluctantly from under his feet.

Investigation became imperative, but following a stumbling trip up a barren hillside of scattered rust-coloured rock to the alleged spot, there was nothing whatever in sight. Alec was indignant at aspersions upon his eyesight so we quartered that area all over again. Sure enough an 'invisible' bird materialized in the centre of the original search area. We had walked by it and close to it a dozen times that morning.

Without a doubt the White-throated Nightjar and its allies represent the ultimate in clever camouflage or 'invisibility' and apart from the chick Alec had seen, there were actually two birds here. At one with their surroundings, these Bronzewing Pigeon-sized birds sat motionless and elongated a few feet apart, right in the open—eyes mere slits in dark brown plumage which was mottled and striped in grey and buff with white throat patches.

Close approach triggered one 'squatter' into rapid zig-zagging flight through the trees, thence again to earth a hundred yards further on, but the second bird rose reluctantly as a last resort, only to 'freeze' on a near-by log the better to observe the fuzzy chick it had left behind.

If possible, this nestless baby represented an even greater triumph of complete mergence with its environment than that achieved by either parent. Shapeless by comparison with most feathered infants (picture), it was as rusty red as the surrounding rocks and every bit as motionless.

Hugh Innes of 'Walla' (Gin Gin) tells me he has seen such fledgeling White-throated Nightjars—which he persists in calling 'white-handled Nightjars'—drop the unbroken stance to make two or three frog-like hops to a new position. Really only their parents could find them. At least the proverbial needle in a haystack would —or should—have a revealing glint!

Towards evening, just at twilight in fact—even before daylight has entirely gone—the two adult Nightjars encountered by Alec Wilson, and which I had met before, take off from these ridges to begin swift and valuable hawking of insects through and high over the treetops.

Three outstanding features of these interesting 'do-gooders' and their colleagues along barren ridges of poor timber—for the species is typical of a lot of range country on and east of the Dividing Range—always impress me.

The first already mentioned is that startling, unheralded, erratic rise from almost underfoot on swift noiseless tapering wings for all the world like the flight of a lone black ghost for whom there is no peace in this wicked old world. Actually these Nightjars frequently give me a start on collecting trips among the poor stony ironbark ranges where I walk daily, collecting not so easily accessible tallow-wood foliage for our koala colony. Though there is nothing to mark their occupancy, the birds are usually about favourite vicinities year in and year out, ever ready to rise from the approach of cattle or human intruders, like rockets from a launching pad.

Whilst stalking a coiled, basking taipan one warm mid-October morning in Wallum country, Kin Kin, Queensland, I well remember the White-throated Nightjar that rose unseen underfoot so abruptly that, tense as I was, my heart literally flew into my throat with it.

Secondly, though quiet over most of the non-breeding months of the year, like many another nocturnal bird, the White-throated Nightjar is a 'joy forever' when it calls by night in its months of excitement and ambition. This winding-up 'song'—three or four mellow repeated up-scale whistles, followed by a rapid chuckle—is sometimes described as unearthly laughter. Actually it is a performance that, heard under the moon on still nights, can only be described as delightfully attractive and cheerfully musical.

To my delight we have one pair of these birds on our own ridge dominating the West Burleigh Sanctuary where they occasionally 'sing' in the evenings.

Thirdly, the reflection of these Nightjar eyes along a spotlight beam produces such astonishing twin coals of fire that the spectacle is almost unbelievable. It still amazes me, though it is many years since I first spotted the phenomenon. That was a night when my spotlight beam picked up a distant reflection atop a forty-foot high dead spar near Mudgeeraba, Queensland. Closer approach revealed the extraordinary glow, ever more pronounced, to emanate from the eyes of a White-throated Nightjar—a frequent experience since, and an indication that tall perches of this type are excellent observation posts for unobstructed sallies.

Three species of these true Nightjars, which comprise a different family (Caprimulgidae) entirely from the Podargidae (Frogmouths) and Owlet Nightjars, belong to Australia but not to Tasmania, as you may have gathered from opening remarks on the White-throated one *(Eurostopodus mystacalis),* they are highly inconspicuous ground roosters and essentially aerial hunters of flying insects, including such obvious ones as 'fire-flies'.

Derivation of the name Caprimulgidae itself is illuminating in its literal interpretation 'of the family of goat-suckers'—a relic of old folklore which held these night flyers responsible for underhanded practices.

One of them, the Large-tailed Nightjar *(Caprimulgus macrurus)* of the Northern Territory to Queensland, at least as far south as Gin Gin, extends also through New Guinea to the Philippines and India. It is non-migratory and famous for its 'chopping' notes, heard persistently through the night.

H. G. Barnard wrote of a single bird which came night after night to his camp on Cape York. It would arrive just after dusk and settle in an exposed place on a projecting bough. Almost as soon as it alighted, it would start the note 'chop! chop! chop!'—about one 'chop' to the second. If an insect flew by the bird darted after it, again returning to the perch where the 'chop! chop! chop!' was resumed. This was kept up the whole evening—the only breaks being for pursuit of food.

Near Cardwell on several occasions, H. G. Barnard saw one of the birds fly to a low horizontal bough where it was joined by its mate. Following this, one would utter a low crooning note, after which the pair would fly away.

When disturbed from the reddish-downed young (for this bird produces a two-egg clutch), the parent birds circle around before alighting on a low limb or log with drooping wings, opening the mouth wide, and uttering a note like the croak of a frog.

From the beginning of August to the end of January, according to this careful observer, the birds call on most nights that weather does not mar. During February, the note only comes at intervals, and from then until August it is seldom heard at all. It is therefore scarcely surprising to find in northern Australia that the Large-tailed Nightjar is also called Axe-bird, Carpenter-bird, Hammer-bird, and also Betting-bird, born of the fact that Australians—by no means backward in such matters—wager on the number of 'chops' that will be uttered between the bird's forays for insects.

Nightjars in general across the world have forced themselves on public attention because of the extraordinary nature and very persistence of their nocturnal vocalism. Most famous perhaps is the American Whip-Poor-Will *(Antrostomus vociferus)* which typically wheels through the air hawking insects, perching at intervals like our Large-tailed Nightjar, to give vent to the 'brain fever' calls from which its popular name is derived.

To maintain contact with one another under obscure conditions, night birds in general are in need of penetrating repetitive vocal signals, and surely a review of these Australian nocturnal calls alone makes it plain that nature has surely obliged.

The third member of the Caprimulgidae, and the last of the owl-like birds on the Australian list, is the Spotted Nightjar *(Eurostopodus guttatus)*. Actually very similar to, and a close relative of the White-throated species, it acts in much the same way, looks the same, but is much more rusty-brown beneath and more profusely spotted above—the latter feature presenting an attractive sight when the bird rises to fly away.

With a somewhat similar series of call notes, interpreted sometimes as 'caw-caw-caw-gobble-gobble-gobble!' it is more a bird of somewhat arid areas west of the Dividing Range. I remember vividly hearing that intriguing night call while camped in the heart of the Victorian Mallee. The bird is nevertheless found at times in dry heathland country on the Pacific and Bass Strait sides of the mountain chain—one instance being at Anglesea and western Port Phillip shores in Victoria where the two species overlap.

In June of 1928 when on a trip to Cape York, H. G. Barnard disturbed a pair of Spotted Nightjars, a pair of White-throated Nightjars and finally a pair of Large-tailed Nightjars, all from the one patch of sandy ground less than three acres in extent, within six miles of the tip of the Cape—a classic case of overlap indeed.

Describing a nocturnal meeting with the Spotted Nightjar along the old Nhill-Murrayville track between Moonlight Tank and Yanac in north-western Victoria, Norman Wakefield noted the powerful eye reflection shared with its White-throated cousin. In the scrubby sand-ridge country comprising the Big Desert this Nightjar was under observation for half an hour and the bird's eyes reflected the car headlights so strongly that its position was visible several hundred yards ahead. It would take to the air and fly off, only to be found progressively several times over, on the road ahead, each time by the intensity of the light beam reflection.

By choice of habitat the species is even more of a ground perching bird than its White-throated near-twin.

Both White-throated and Spotted Nightjars are one-egg birds, making no attempt at any form of nest. The egg itself is a work of art in the line of protective concealment—in the case of the White-throated species having a buff, stone or cream-coloured background carrying black and bluish-grey markings and again one is inclined to astonishment that, once having flown off, the bird itself can ever

Indignant family! Frogmouth mother (right) and two fledglings five weeks old endeavour to bluff an intruder with clapping beaks, gaping yellow mouths, and harsh cries.

'Camouflage plus': Tawny Frogmouth's back view as it perches stiffened out on the approach of intruders.

Frogmouths may be weak-footed, but there is power in their massive beaks. Rats and mice, frogs and small birds, if captured on the ground, are later beaten to pulp against a limb. Two birds argue about possession of a mouse.

The large grey bird mistakenly known to the casual observer and most country dwellers as the Mopoke or Frogmouth 'owl'. Actually the Tawny Frogmouth is a king-sized Nightjar, and is here pictured brooding eggs on a ground level nest (a most unusual site).

'Tiny, 8½ inch long cousin of the Frogmouths is likewise not an owl but superficially so like one that it is named Owlet Nightjar.' Often referred to as Fairy or Moth 'owl', its call note is a weird sighing 'chirr . . . chirr'.

Fledgling White-throated Nightjar. 'Shapeless by comparison with most feathered infants, it was as rusty red as the surrounding rocks and every bit as motionless . . . the nestless baby represents a great triumph of complete mergence with environment.'

White-throated Nightjar and chick, West Burleigh hills. 'Sure enough an "invisible" bird materialized in the centre of the original search area. We'd walked by it and close to it a dozen times that morning.' The fledgling squats in front of the mother in the geometrical centre of the picture. In courting procedure adults fly by night, clicking beaks and crooning continuously.

Single egg of White-throated Nightjar in situ on dry ridge near Nambucca River, northern New South Wales, 18 December 1946. Buff, stone or cream coloured with black daubings and underlying markings of bluish grey, it is far less conspicuous than represented here in the black and white picture. Photo Merv Goddard.

possibly relocate its treasure. Disturbed from the egg in Mallee eucalypt country, hen Spotted Nightjars may fly thirty feet or more with an ensuing several steps after-landing move before lowering the head and raising the tail some five or six inches above ground level. 'Freezing' thus in a kind of Frogmouth-in-reverse attitude, the Nightjar is just another piece of 'tree litter'—so fantastically blended with the landscape as to be invisible immediately one's eyes leave it momentarily.

One thing very certain is that Nightjars can have little betraying scent. Despite their ground dwelling habits, bushfires, vulnerability to obliteration by foxes and native predators, they continue to flourish as long as their habitats remain inviolate.

Fortunately for them they so often favour such poor, scraggly, uninviting, unproductive country with which avaricious man can do nothing, that they remain undisturbed to carry on their quiet and effective insect patrols with no more bother than an occasional daylight move ahead of wandering cattle.

Nomenclature

ORDER STRIGIFORMES (Nocturnal Birds of Prey)
FAMILY STRIGIDAE
Ninox strenua Gould

Ninox rufa rufa (Gould)
N. rufa marginata Mees
N. rufa queenslandica Mathews
N. rufa humeralis Bonaparte
N. rufa aruensis Schlegel

Ninox connivens connivens (Latham)
N. connivens peninsularis Salvadori
N. connivens occidentalis Ramsay
N. connivens assimilis Salvadori & d'Albertis
N. connivens rufostrigata G. R. Gray

Ninox novaeseelandiae novaeseelandiae (J. F. Gmelin)
N. novaeseelandiae leucopsis (Gould)
N. novaeseelandiae boobook (Latham)
N. novaeseelandiae rufigaster Mees
N. novaeseelandiae lurida de Vis
N. novaeseelandiae halmaturina Mathews
N. novaeseelandiae undulata (Latham)
N. novaeseelandiae albaria Ramsay
N. novaeseelandiae ocellata (Bonaparte)
N. novaeseelandiae melvillensis Mathews
N. novaeseelandiae pusilla Mayr & Rand
N. novaeseelandiae remigialis Stresemann
N. novaeseelandiae cinnamomina Hartert
N. novaeseelandiae moae Mayr
N. novaeseelandiae fusca Vieillot
N. novaeseelandiae plesseni Stresemann

158

FAMILY TYTONIDAE

Tyto alba delicatula Gould

Tyto novaehollandiae novaehollandiae (Stephens)

T. novaehollandiae castanops (Gould)

T. novaehollandiae galei Mathews

T. novaehollandiae melvillensis Mathews

T. novaehollandiae kimberli Mathews

Tyto longimembris longimembris (Jerdon)

Tyto longimembris papuensis Hartert

Tyto tenebricosa tenebricosa (Gould)

T. tenebricosa multipunctata Mathews

T. tenebricosa arfaki (Schlegel)

ORDER CORACIIFORMES (which includes Frogmouths and Night-
    jars)

FAMILY PODARGIDAE

Podargus strigoides strigoides (Latham)

P. strigoides phalaenoides Gould

P. strigoides brachypterus Gould

P. strigoides gouldi Masters

P. strigoides victoriae Mathews

P. strigoides cornwalli Mathews

P. strigoides cuvieri Vigors & Horsfield

Podargus papuensis Quoy & Gaimard

Podargus ocellatus marmoratus Gould

Podargus plumiferus—synonym for *P. ocellatus marmoratus* Gould

FAMILY AEGOTHELIDAE

Aegotheles cristatus cristatus (J. White)

Aegotheles cristatus leucogaster Gould

FAMILY CAPRIMULGIDAE

Eurostopodus mystacalis Temminck

E. guttatus guttatus (Vigors & Horsfield)

Caprimulgus macrurus yorki Mathews

Index

160

Daylesford 2, 63
De Courtenay, Bob 113
Delicate Owl *see* Barn Owl
Dowse, F. R. 116

egg sizes, comparative 99, 141
'Elizabeth' 83
Elliott, A. J. 117
Elwood, W. H. 10
Emu 37, 38, 71, 85, 117, 126, 147
'Essie' 10–11
Eurostopodus guttatus 155
E. mystacalis 154

Fairy Owl *see* Owlet Nightjar
Favaloro, N. J. 40, 99, 121, 122, 141
'Ferox' 9–11, 14, 16–19
Fleay, M. Glover 9
Frogmouth 143

Gallagher, Paul 68–9
George, G. 124
Ghost Bird *see* Barn Owl
Giovine, L. 102
Goddard, Merv 44, 50–1, 58, 60, 62, 63,
    66, 78, 79, 99, 106, 126, 127–8, 130–3,
    134, 136–40
Goodisson, J. R. 75, 77, 79
Gould, John 4, 43, 113, 115–6
Grass Owl 123–8
    appearance 123–4, 127
    camouflage 123–4
    eggs 123, 141
    feeding habits 128
    flight 125, 127–8
    habitat 123, 124
    nesting habits 126, 127
    owlets 125
    size (comparative) of male and female
        124
    squats 125, 126, 127–8
Great European Owl 40

H. L. White collection 37, 66
Hammer-bird *see* Large-tailed Nightjar
Hartley's Creek Sanctuary 126
Hawk Owl *see* Strigidae
Healesville Sanctuary 36, 38, 109, 116
Hindwood, Keith 149, 150
'Hookie' 32–4, 42
Horned Owl 40, 73
Howe, F. 37, 130
'Hughie' 98–9

Hyem, E. L. 132-3, 134, 140

Innes, Hugh 76, 125, 153

Jahn, Ben 8

Kelly, Vincent 14–15
Korweingeboora 4, 6, 13

Labbett, W. 2–8
Large-tailed Nightjar 154–6
Le Souef, D. 15
Leach, Dr J. A. 10
Lee, Miss A. 116
Lewis, F. 15, 38
'Little Mattie' 98–9
Long Shanks Owl *see* Grass Owl

'Mac' 55–7
McLennan's Creek 44, 50
McMillan, Dudley 109, 110
Marbled Frogmouth 149, 150
Masked Owl 16, 100, 112–22
    eggs 141
    habitat 112
    see also Barn Owl, Grass Owl, Sooty
        Owl, Tasmanian Masked Owl
Mathews 67
Mayr, Ernst 86, 103, 150
Mees, Dr G. F. 49, 66, 67, 72, 86, 113
Melbourne Zoo 15, 16, 109, 144, 146
mice plagues 104
Monkey-faced Owl *see* Masked Owl
Moorabool Reservoir 2
Mopoke *see* Boobook Owl
Morepork *see* Boobook Owl
Moth Owl *see* Owlet Nightjar
Mount Cole 8, 10, 13
Mount Riddell 36, 38
Mount Tool-be-wong 38
Mus musculus 104

Nightjar *see* Frogmouth
Ninox connivens 40, 58, 71–84
N. connivens connivens 72
Ninox novaeseelandiae boobook 72, 90, 99
N. novaeseelandiae leucopsis 86
N. novaeseelandiae lurida 86
N. novaeseelandiae novaeseelandiae 86
N. novaeseelandiae ocellata 86
Ninox rufa 20, 58, 64–70
N. rufa marginata 66–7
N. rufa queenslandica 67
N. rufa rufa 66